No Firmer Foundation

Growing Up in Ashfield in the Mid-Twentieth Century

Bob Bates

iUniverse, Inc.
New York   Bloomington

No Firmer Foundation
Growing Up in Ashfield in the Mid-Twentieth Century

iUniverse books may be ordered through booksellers or by contacting:

iUniverse
1663 Liberty Drive
Bloomington, IN 47403
www.iuniverse.com
1-800-Authors (1-800-288-4677)

Because of the dynamic nature of the Internet, any Web addresses or links contained in this book may have changed since publication and may no longer be valid.

ISBN: 978-1-4401-5147-7 (sc)
ISBN: 978-1-4401-5148-4 (ebk)

Library of Congress Control Number: 2009930576

Printed in the United States of America

iUniverse rev. date: 6/15/2009

This book is dedicated to the strong and stalwart Ashfield oaks under whose protective canopy we grew and flourished. My mom and dad were two of my oaks, and there were others – neighbors, teachers, clergymen, countless more. This book is dedicated to them, the mighty Ashfield oaks, now fallen, for their lifetime of quiet but firm support.

Contents

Acknowledgements

This book was begun in 1996 in response to a request from my daughter, Robyn, (and seconded by my son, Don) to share something of my past with them. It has grown by fits and starts in its nearly thirteen year gestation, and there have been many people who have stepped forward offering encouragement, commentary and material.

Above all else, I owe a huge appreciation to Sharon, my wife of forty-four years, for her patience and understanding. Particularly during the past three years, I have spent countless hours in the den at the keyboard, creating, organizing and reworking what you see before you now, and she has quietly awaited its completion.

Sharon and Doreen Rossi, our friend of many years, reviewed the early efforts. I thank them for their questions, counsel, and suggestions. One result of these two city girls' proofreading was the surfacing of lots of farm terms that I'd never thought to question.

In addition, in the several years I've labored over this work, Shirley Scott, my sister; Dot Townsley, my mother, now deceased; and Aunt Martha Townsley have been instrumental in clarifying some of my memories that had become hazy. They have as well been able add flesh and substance to some of the things of which I'd only known the barest details, and to them, I owe the deepest of thanks.

Special thanks goes to Alden Gray for his early encouragement, and to Nancy Garvin, a friend who urged me to publish this work and read, edited and critiqued each chapter as it emerged. Nancy's advice and counsel have been indispensable.

Heart-felt thanks is offered to everyone who provided key information - Bill Craft, Ruth Craft, Charlie Groff, Bud Scott, Fred Scott, Betty (Mislak) Sylvester, Bill Townsley, Ray Townsley, Russ Williams, and others.

Many thanks go to the persons whose photographs appear in this book. Don Bates, Aunt Martha Townsley and Betsey Lyman graciously permitted me to use their work. Thanks also goes to my mom and the several unknown photographers of long ago who captured a way of life we look back on now with fondness.

Bob Bates

Finally, a special debt of gratitude goes to the "Review Crew", Doreen Rossi, Karen Moreau, Carole Thorp, and Robyn Descoteau for their diligent and thorough work in helping to make this book more readable.

Bob Bates
Nashua, New Hampshire
May 2009

Donald N. Bates photo

Introduction

The village of Ashfield lies in the Berkshire hills and valleys of western Massachusetts. It was established as *Huntstown* in 1769 through a land grant from the Massachusetts legislature to the survivors and their heirs of Captain Ephraim Hunt's company of Indian fighters of the 1700s. The town became *Ashfield* soon after its founding and flourished briefly in the mid 1800s as a producer of mint. By the middle of the 1900s Ashfield had become a community of dairy farmers and lumbermen.

I am blessed to have been born in Ashfield and had the great fortune to have been raised in Ashfield. Though addresses have changed over the years since, a big part of me still lives in Ashfield. I am an Ashfielder.

My memories of Ashfield begin in the early 1940s in Apple Valley, the northwest corner of the town, where I was raised on the Townsley farm. Life in this New England hill town was often hard and unforgiving, but life here could be full of beauty, laughter, joy and fellowship. Nothing could have provided me a firmer foundation for life in the real world of the last part of the twentieth century and the beginning of the twenty-first.

To understand my perspective and points of view in the comments in this volume, it may help to understand something of my upbringing.

I am the son of Lewis Edward and Dorothy (Nelson) Bates, then of Bellus Road in Baptist Corner. My dad was the son of Ceylon (pronounced "SEE-l'n") and Ethel (Rice) Bates of Smith Road in Ashfield. He had two older sisters, Marjorie and Florence, and all three were schooled at the Apple Valley district school and at Sanderson Academy. Ceylon was originally from Cummington, and Ethel was one of a large family of Rices who had long called Ashfield home. It's through Lewis and Orpha (Sanderson) Rice's daughters that many of Ashfield's larger families are related: Jeannette "Nettie" Rice married Clarence Hall, Grace Rice married Raymond Howes, and Ethel Rice married Ceylon Bates. In addition, son Frank Rice and his wife Grace lived in town. Son Pliny and daughter Sophronia Gertrude, known as "Gert," were childless.

The Bates Farm on Smith Hill, later Ad Graves'. Behind it is Smith's Farm, later Richard and Mary Hall's. House to the right is Harry Graves'. About 1918.
Unknown Photographer, Author's collection.

Dorothy, my mom, was born in Haverhill, Massachusetts, the eldest daughter of Ernest and Mabel Rebecca (Bartlett) Nelson. She was raised with her younger sister, Florence, in Goshen, New Hampshire, and nearby towns. A 1937 graduate of Worcester State Teachers College, she was the only one of her class to land a job right away in that Great Depression year.

Ernest Nelson, "Gramp" to his grandchildren, came from Goshen, New Hampshire, the youngest of four brothers. Mabel Nelson, "Nannie" as we called her, was raised in Haverhill, Massachusetts. They were married at Haverhill in 1914.

Mother's first job was teaching a junior high school class in Cummington. She boarded with Rollin and Nellie Bates of Cummington, as was customary for young single female teachers of the day. One day a handsome and eligible bachelor nephew of Mr. Bates brought his Mom to visit her brother-in-law's family. Mother reported it was love at first sight. She and Lewis were married in Groveland, Massachusetts, in November, 1938.

My dad and mom, Lewis and Dorothy, owned the dairy farm on Bellus Road in Ashfield now owned and operated by Tom and Cynthia Cranston and their family. By all accounts it was a prosperous farm. By area definition, *prosperous* meant that at the end of the year you had more money in your pockets than at the same time the year before.

Lewis died suddenly of a stroke on May 26, 1941, a scant two weeks before his 30th birthday, leaving his grieving mom, his distraught wife and a six-month-old son. My mom had been thoroughly impressed by the people of Ashfield in her short life as Mrs. Bates. People like Fran Gray, Theresa Eldridge, Mary Priscilla Howes, my dad's family and members of the Grange, of which my dad had been Master, all had drawn her close in her grief following my dad's death.

At first, many neighbors pitched in to do chores and otherwise help out. But as time wore on, Mother and Gramma (Ethel) Bates concluded that it wasn't practical for a young woman with an infant child to operate the farm alone. Mother sold the farm, livestock and equipment, and moved for a short time to Norwell, where her mom and dad, Ernest and Mabel Nelson, were then living.

The lure of Ashfield, with its warm neighbors and supportive community, pulled Mother back. In late 1941, she learned of the availability of the Leland Wheeler farm in Apple Valley, just down the road from the Townsley's farm, and bought it in January 1942 with part of the proceeds from the sale of the Bellus Road farm. Mother and her parents moved in, then she turned the farm over to her dad to operate. Gramp Nelson had been a farm laborer all his life thus far. This became his first opportunity to work a place of his own. He raised chickens.

The Nelsons - and the young and attractive Widow Bates, now 26 - bought milk from Townsleys. Most days Gramp walked the quarter mile or so to Townsleys to get the milk – but once in a while, the shy but handsome Preston Townsley, then 32, walked the quarter mile to Nelsons. One thing lead to another, and Mother and Pres were married on February 8, 1943, by Rev. Walter Couch of the Ashfield Congregational Church. Soon thereafter I was moved a short distance up the road to the Townsley farm.

"The shy but handsome Preston Townsley," about 1943.
Unknown Photographer, Author's collection.

Preston Williams Townsley was the eldest of the four children of Fred and Alta (Williams) Townsley. Preston's brother, Harold, was by all accounts a gifted scholar and inventor. An Army Air Corps Lieutenant and navigator, he was **declared** missing and presumed dead over the Bay of Biscay in World War II. His brother, Floyd, was a career Army officer who, with his wife, Jane and their youngsters, often summered at the farm between assignments. Ralph, the youngest brother, was a dairyman, and with his wife, Martha, became a fixture in Ashfield life. Many of us have happily relaxed over a cup of coffee, conversation – and sometimes *inspiration* at the Townsley Farm's kitchen table.

Preston preferred that we kids call him "Pres," though my sister, Shirley, often called him "Daddy."

Pres was a larger than life figure for my earliest years. It was hard for me to approach him and talk to him, and now in looking back I know he was incredibly shy. Not only that, but he was very soft-spoken, to the point that I sometimes could only guess at what he said. Early on, guessing didn't work too well, as I'd often head off in the wrong direction or start to do what I *thought* he said, and that resulted in his ire – and frustration.

As I grew older I came to respect Pres for the values he passed on, for the understanding of work, for the ability to work hard, and for patience.

Pres, by instilling in me an appreciation of work, gave me perhaps the most valuable gift of my life: by working harder or longer (or both!) than others enabled me to move ahead faster, often with less book-learning.

Some well-meaning people have pitied me that my own dad died when I was six months old, long before I knew him. To the contrary, I've long considered that I had not one dad, as most people do, but three and perhaps four fathers. My dad, Lewis Edward Bates, gave me life. Stepfather Preston Townsley, from whom most of my "father figure" came from him, taught me how to work. Gramp Nelson taught me moderation and family love. Pete Bundy, perhaps more a big brother than father, showed me that I could enjoy these things!

As a young fiancé and husband, I proudly introduced Sharon, my bride, to Ashfield in the mid-1960s. From time to time in this book I'll mention her and our children, Robyn and Donald, who spent most of their summers with Gram and Gramp Townsley and the Townsley cousins. And indeed, Don and his family have settled in Ashfield, continuing a hundred-year Bates presence in the town.

Bob Bates
Nashua, New Hampshire
May 2009

Chapter 1
Townsley Farm
The Farmhouse

Townsley Farm sits astride Apple Valley Road in Ashfield about a mile into the valley from Route 112. To most outsiders, the white farmhouse and sturdy outbuildings suddenly appear, framed by the many willows and the ghost of an ancient black cherry that guard the bridge across Clessons Brook. Hilly fields surround the farm buildings, and apple orchards work up the side of the valley toward the forested Pumpkin Hill. Clessons Brook, "Apple Valley brook" to most of us, tumbles out of the hills to the north and west.

Townsley Farm in late May, 1958. Grammie Townsley's favorite black cherry tree spreads over the bridge. By late summer the tiny, bitter cherries dropped onto the pavement, where they were crushed by traffic and gave off an acrid fruity odor.
Dorothy N. Townsley Photo, Author's collection.

The older farm buildings date from the late 1870s. The farm house is more recent, raised in 1910 to replace its predecessor which was destroyed by fire in 1909, the same year my step-dad, Preston Townsley, was born. The present configuration with the milking parlor and pole barn came about in 1958.

The Townsley farmhouse was a two-story, slate-roofed structure with a cellar beneath. Downstairs, where Fred and Grammie lived, there were a kitchen, bath, dining room, living room, and two bedrooms, though one was so small that it was little more than a storage closet. In addition, there was "the Back Room" and a milkroom that were more adjuncts of the farm than the farmhouse.

The upstairs apartment contained a kitchen, living room and four bedrooms, as well as a sunny but unheated fully enclosed porch. An inside stairway at the east end connected the two apartments. A second, outside stairway wound up and around the northwest corner to a door on the enclosed porch.

After they were married in 1943, Pres, Mother and I moved into the upstairs apartment, and before long, my sister, Shirley, was born.

For most of my childhood my bedroom was at northeast corner of the second floor of the farmhouse, at the top of the stairway between the first and second floor. It was a refuge where I could dream, and at various times it was a fort, a landing field for my model airplanes, my own independent country (I even wrote my own Constitution!). It was often a mess, and Mother and I would often wage war over its cleanliness and orderliness. Her definition and mine often differed.

At the east corner, past the top of the stairs, was the spacious guest room, and from time to time, Pres' bedroom. The room faces down the road toward the bridge, and is bright and sunny and cheerful. Uncle Floyd and Aunt Jane Townsley usually stayed here when they visited, on leave from the Army, during the summer.

Next along the front of the house was another bright, sun-filled bedroom. Pres and Mother slept here until he moved over to the guest room. This room also faces down the valley, and it was from here about three o'clock on a dark early March morning in 1957 that Mother awoke to see a blaze at Gramp and Nannie's. The barn Gramp had just finished cleaning out in preparation for the next flock of chickens was thoroughly involved. All the Ashfield firemen could do was to wet down the main barn to prevent it from catching on as well.

Most of the time these two big bedrooms saw pleasanter sights: the rising sun lifting the fog out of the valley below, the pine-shaded Picnic Place across the bridge up to the left, Ridge Hill in the distance – and sweeter sounds, like the first robins and phoebes announcing the arrival of spring, and distant crows heralding the start of the day's foraging.

Shirley's room was just across the hallway from Mother's doorway. It had been my bedroom when I first arrived as a toddler, and Shirley was given

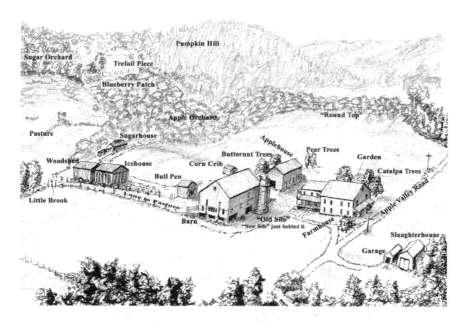

Townsley Farm about 1950, looking northwest.
Author's sketch.

the room when she became old enough. It was small, and faced toward Roundtop across a large hayfield.

The upstairs bathroom featured a claw-footed cast iron tub. A short chest of drawers, holding all the bath linens, stood in front to the window, and a wall-mounted medicine cabinet held all the family's collection of aspirin, antihistamines – and Rawleigh's Anti-pain Oil.

Anti-Pain Oil[1], a liniment by design, was the universal antidote for any kind of bug bite or sting. Applied soon after the sting, Anti-Pain Oil burned warmly, but we knew that soon it would begin its cooling healing, especially when Mom or Nannie would "Foo it, Mommy, foo it" to hasten the cooling.

---

1 On a whim I ordered some Anti-Pain Oil in 2007 from a website ($10 for an 8 oz. bottle), and though the smell was close, it's not as sharp as either Shirley or remembered.

It was remarkable to Shirley and me for its aroma: it sang of stopping the sting and of healing hugs and cooing sympathy.

Our living room was truly the room in which we relaxed as a family. Two windows faced south across the farmyard and down the valley. Between the windows was a table on which was a shaded lamp, and in the drawer under the top was the family's growing collection of photographs. On a lower shelf, under the drawer, stood a pile of recent *Recorder-Gazette* newspapers and *National Geographics* and *Ladies Home Journals*.

Atop the table, too, was the family telephone. Everyone in the lower end of Apple Valley was on the same party line, but our service was pretty much automatic. Everybody had identical black Western Electric dial telephones. You picked up the hand set, listened to see if anyone was talking, and if not, dialed the number of the person you wanted.

The table was flanked by Preston's Chair to the left and Mother's Chair to the right. Preston's Chair always had a hassock in front of it. On the end of the table next to his chair sat Preston's ash tray – or *pipe tray*, more aptly. It was brass and it clanged mightily as he knocked stale tobacco from his pipe bowl.

Behind Mother's Chair was a closet which held the family games, Monopoly, Parcheesi, Authors and that mysterious Ouija board that neither Shirley nor I could figure out.

A couch with wooden armrests and three floppy pillow cushions graced the wall next to the bathroom. This was where I read "Lightfoot, the Deer," Jimmy Skunk and others of the Thornton W. Burgess classic "Mother West Wind" series.

A single north window faced across the garden and on toward Roundtop. Under the window sat a table; it was usually covered with whatever Mother's current hobby happened to be – African violets or tropical fish most often.

Farther along the north wall sat the upright piano. We acquired this relic saved from Charlie Nadeau's fire in the summer of 1955, and it always smelled faintly of smoke. Mother insisted that Shirley and I have piano lessons, and we duly joined Winnie Field's sizeable group of students as we banged away at the keyboard. Grammie Townsley, who lived downstairs, never complained (that I know of) of the noise. Most of Mrs. Field's students were girls, which wasn't so bad for this early pubescent teenager, but I thought I'd rather play baseball, so I opted out after a year or so.

If we relaxed as a family in the living room, then we lived as a family in the kitchen. Here we ate, we talked, and very infrequently, we held our family meetings.

Mother cooked with wood on a large black cast iron kitchen range. In the early 1950s we acquired a combination wood and electric stove. It was white except for the smaller end that could be fired with wood, which was black. It took up about the same room as the old wood range, and size-wise, about two thirds of it was electric. The rationale, as it was explained to me, was that if the electricity went off, you could still get by using the end of the

Townsley Farm, from the Picnic Place, about 1930. Pumpkin Hill is in the background, and the apple orchard creeps up its side. Roundtop is the extreme right, and Scott's is just beyond it. Apple Valley Road sweeps by, left to right at the bottom. The driveway swings in front of the white house and on between the barn at the left and the applehouse at the right behind the house. Three chicken coops are at the left, below the barn; behind it is the tin-roofed bull pen. The structure partially hidden behind the barn may be a henhouse.
Unknown Photographer, Author's Collection.

stove that burned wood. Really, I think, neither Pres nor Mother, nor the very influential Grammie Townsley downstairs, fully trusted electricity yet.

Because we cooked (and heated) with wood, somebody had to replenish the wood supply. Stovewood as well as chunk wood for furnace was stored in the cellar, so somebody had to lug the stovewood to the stoves in which it would be consumed.

In our second floor kitchen we had a cut-down oil barrel as a "woodbox," tucked away behind the stove. It was my job to fill the woodbox. There was nothing even remotely glorious about this task – it was just plain hard grunt work. You trudged downstairs into the cellar, gathered up an armload of wood, struggled up the cellar stairs then up the back stairs to the second floor, across the porch and into the kitchen to drop the armload into the woodbox. If you worked it right, that first arm load of wood made a satisfying "Clang" when you dropped it into that nearly empty tin woodbox.

If those back stairs were icy, and they often were, the trek over them could be an adventure. One frosty morning in her haste to catch the school bus, Shirley slipped and thumped and bumped down them. She just picked herself up and ran along.

I happened to think just now of the old Yankee term, "Sick abed of the woodbox." It was a response to, "How're you feeling?" and meant, "I'm feeling kind of poorly, but I'm well enough to have my bed near the woodbox so I can get up and feed the fire." And it might be a welcome response if you'd been really laid up for a while.

Behind the woodbox was a collection of wooden yardsticks, and these most often served as instruments of discipline. If Shirley or I ever acted up, all Mother had to do was rattle a yardstick against the metal woodbox, and the inferred threat got our acts together in pretty short order. By the way, I don't remember that she actually ever had to apply the yardsticks to our behinds, but I expect she must have at least once.

The clothes washing machine sat in a corner behind the range. Perhaps a Maytag, it too, was electric. It had a sizeable tub with an agitator, and a wringer that could be swung out over a nearby washtub if needed. Mother, more than once, jawed angrily at some article of clothing getting wrapped around the wringer. To the best of my knowledge, she never got any body parts, other than an occasional pinched finger, caught in the wringer.

A porcelain double sink sat under a window facing south over the farm yard. We had three faucets at the sink. Besides the usual hot and cold water spigots, we had a third faucet just for spring water, same as in Grammie Townsley's kitchen downstairs, and in the Back Room where we washed out the milking equipment.

Our kitchen table most often sat in the middle of the kitchen. Occasionally, during the summer when it was hot, Mother moved the kitchen table in front of the double windows that faced north over the garden, past the pear trees and on up towards Roundtop.

Most meals were taken together as a family, Mother and Pres at the ends of the table, Shirley and me at the sides. The exception was breakfast. Shirley and I wolfed down cereal and milk, then either washed dishes or made beds before dashing off to wait for the school bus. Mother usually had a cup of coffee and a piece of toast after we left. Pres had eaten and left – for the woods or whatever - often before Shirley and I were up.

While some farms (Gramp Nelson's for one) still had iceboxes, we had a Gibson electric refrigerator. Our refrigerator had a tip-out compartment at the bottom, and here we stored all the breakfast cereals – Corn Flakes, Wheaties and Grape Nut Flakes.

Cereal was covered with raw whole milk – or top-of-the-milk. We used maple syrup as the sweetener of choice (in the years we were still making it) rather than white granulated stuff. The philosophy was, I suppose, that if you made syrup it didn't cost you anything. I also suppose it never dawned on anyone that one could have sold the syrup and used the money to buy sweetener.

My favorite cereals were Nabisco Shredded Wheat, maybe only because they had those great Straight Arrow cards inside, and Shredded Ralston, which sponsored the Tom Mix radio show about supper time (Shredded Ralston's radio jingle urged, "Take a tip from Tom, go and tell your mom, 'Shredded Ralston can't be beat.'" It didn't rhyme as well when Shredded Ralston became Wheat Chex).

On a commode[2] near the twin north windows was the family radio. Here Shirley and I listened for the miraculous, like "No school today in Ashfield," and the mundane, like the every-suppertime adventures of *Straight Arrow* and *Tom Mix* and others. Every evening we would arrange our chores around their nightly episodes and those of *Sergeant Preston of the Yukon* and *Clyde Beatty*.

The last room on our tour of the second floor is a very sunny porch, with windows on all three sides and a door to the outside staircase. It was most pleasant here in the summer. Mother used it as a nursery first for me, then for Shirley, then later for a large brood of African Violets that she grew from leaf slips cut from other plants. It was from here I watched the building of the first silo, the one that would later challenge my confidence.

The outside stairs began with a landing just outside the door on the north side of the porch, ran down to a second landing well up the wall of the milk room, then ending near the door to the milk room.

Along the side of the farmhouse, at the corner nearest the barn, was a poured concrete porch. In front of the Back Room and outside the kitchen, it sheltered the doorways to the Back Room and to Grammie and Fred's kitchen.

At the barn end of the porch grew an amazing and tenacious trumpet vine. It crept and wound around everything it could reach, despite our harsh New England winters. It harbored ants and spiders, and when it blossomed, it attracted hummingbirds as well as bees and hornets. How that plant flourished! Given full sun, well-manured soil, and with what the trumpet vine took to be freedom to roam, it rapidly crept up the two nearby columns and was on its way over the porch roof when somebody decided it was well

---

2 A "Commode" is a piece of ornate furniture – a chest of drawers or enclosed shelves. "Commode's" association with toilet is a twentieth century adaptation

past time to cut it down. However, cutting it down proved to be but a minor setback for that hardy trumpet vine. Before the summer was over, impudent new tentacles had sprouted from the roots, and the cycle began to repeat. Today, despite numerous attempts on its life, that embattled trumpet vine still lives!

The "milk room," actually a milk storage facility, with the porch above it, was an addition in the late 1930s, I believe, from pictures from Preston's collection. The milk room was equipped with a water-filled, refrigerated cooler, into which one could place perhaps a dozen forty quart milk cans. In addition, there was an overflow tank in front, always full of the chilled overflow from the big cooler.

As a young fishermen and fledgling naturalist, I found the overflow tank to be a dandy place to put the trout I had just caught at the bridge below the farm. If I hustled, and the trout hadn't been badly hooked, the fish would survive and even thrive in the overflow tank, though they must have been bewildered at the sudden change in surroundings. I could watch the little trout as they circled the tank, but better still, I could show off my trophy catches to the Greenman cousins and cousin Bill Townsley.

At one point I had three or four little brook trout in the tank. I learned the trout liked worms (duh!), which meant grabbing a shovel and digging up some worms. But they also liked hamburg, and it was awful easy because we had hamburg often in its various guises. Just pinch some off from what's in the refrigerator and toss it into the tank.

What puzzled me about my trout laboratory was that the trout would last only a few days in the tank before they would disappear without a trace. One day I was working in the applehouse where I could look out at the milkroom door, and there was Peter, one of our housecats, catching his paw around the corner of the door and, with little effort, letting himself in. I watched intently as Peter hunkered down on the edge of the tank and intently watched as the trout lazily circled the tank. As the fish circled near the top, Peter scooped it out with his paw onto the milkroom floor. He pounced on it and in a flash, gulped it down without leaving a trace - save for a puddle of water swiftly drying in the summer heat!

Next inside the milkroom was "the Back Room." It was directly beneath the upstairs kitchen, and served as a mud-room, with coats and hats hung on the wall, and shoes and boots lined up near the door. Here was the wood-fired hot water heater and another woodbox to be filled. A large black sink sat in the corner, at which Grammie Townsley washed out the Surge milking machines twice a day. Back in an alcove next to the milkroom was a large upright freezer. The freezer had heavy insulated double doors, and the shelves inside each had a door. The whole family stored frozen items there. Ours were on the right side, Ralph's were on the left, and Grammie's were there, too, though I can't remember where.

The family gun collection hung on the the Back Room walls nearest the barn. The collection at that time was a couple of shotguns, two or three rifles and a couple of handguns, all hung in gun cases or holsters.

Hunting and firearms were part of the way of life in 1950s western Massachusetts hill towns. It was commonplace to hear gunshots echoing up and down Apple Valley at any time of the year, but most often in the fall during the hunting seasons.

We understood that the firearms were off limits to us youngsters. Though the firearms weren't under lock and key that I remember, I knew I'd be in big trouble if I touched them. And I never fired a piece until after I had taken the required Rod and Gun Club Hunter Safety course at the Ashfield Firehouse the fall before I was 16.

The downstairs kitchen was large and bright. It had the usual accouterments, a large double sink – with hot, cold *and* spring water faucets, an electric kitchen range and a small kitchen table. But what fascinated me most was the refrigerator. It was tiny by today's standards, and stood off the floor on four legs. Atop the icebox was the compressor assembly (and they were referred to as "iceboxes" long after the dawning of electric refrigerators).

Charlie Groff also grew up on the Townsley Farm. His perspective goes back about ten years earlier than my memory horizon. He remembered in a letter of March 2009, "Six to eight hired hands worked the farm in the late 1930s and early 1940s. Every work day at about ten in the morning, Mother T. [Grammie Townsley] would stand outside the house on the open porch and clang the large bronze bell. The hired men would come running from every farm work site to enjoy the morning respite of cider and home made doughnuts.

"A man appeared one day for the morning bread. Nobody recognized him.

"'Who be you?' asked Mother T.

"'I am from the Clark farm,' he replied.

"'Enjoy the day,' she glared. 'I shan't see you again!'"

Off the kitchen was the large sunny dining room. Here was a large dining table and matching chairs. With the leaves in, it could seat eight or ten people. With one or more card tables set up in the living room (where us kids were seated so as not to disturb the adults at the big table), another half dozen people, kids usually, could be accommodated. We kids looked forward to the day when we would be admitted to the circle of adults at the big table, and it was a rite of passage to be permitted to sit at the Adults Table.

Most of the time the dining room was set up as a sitting room. Grammie sat in a large Morris[3] chair in the corner where she could see all that went on outside as she worked at her crocheting.

Grammie and Fred's bathroom was at the north side of the house. The toilet was very near the window, and I imagine even Fred might stare out the window at the growing garden.

Next along the north wall was Grammie and Fred's bedroom and a small room with one door to the larger bedroom on one end and another that opened to the foyer at the east end of the house.

At the southeast corner of the house, directly below the guest bedroom on the second floor, was the living room. It was here that Floyd set up the first television set about 1953.

A centerpiece of the farm, during the summer months, at least, was the front porch. The north side was windowed, but the eastern and southern exposures were screened. It spanned the width of the house and looked over Apple Valley Road. In the front of the porch a large Japanese quince blossomed lustily early every summer.

Under the shade of a Japanese Walnut tree and one of the four Northern Catalpas that stood guard over the farmhouse, the front porch was always cool on a hot summer day. Beneath the glass windows on the north side was a double bed. Pres slept here during summer months, as did his nephew, Roland, later on. There was a random collection of wicker and other chairs, and a couple of small tables as well. It was here that Pres taught [cousin] Bill and me how to play cribbage.

Cribbage is a fun card game in a family heirloom sort of way. From my vantage point now of nearly seventy years, I see cribbage as a bond that connects many generations and cultures, a communion kind of thing: here sit I, playing a game that my fathers and grandfathers for many generations have played, following the same rules, with the same joys and frustrations.

---

3 Wikipedia, the Internet's "free encyclopedia," reports, *"A **Morris Chair** is an early type of reclining chair. It was first marketed around 1866 in England [and has been widely copied since], the design features a seat with a reclining back and moderately high armrests, which give the chair an old-style appearance. The characteristic feature of a Morris chair is a hinged back, set between two un-upholstered arms, with the reclining angle adjusted through a row of pegs, holes or notches in each arm."* Grammie T's Morris chair had dark stained woodwork and brown leather cushions. Pres claimed it after her death (I doubt Floyd and Ralph fought him very hard!), and fell asleep in it most evenings well before prime time on TV. Most of us found it most uncomfortable!

As you learn to play cribbage, there's an epiphany where all of a sudden you understand how to combine your four cards to count points at the end of a hand. I had a collection of fours and fives and sixes, one that a seasoned player could glance at and say, "That's twenty four – fifteen eight plus a double double run." In my youthful exuberance, I dashed off to show Pres my gold mine. I excitedly counted off about fifteen twelve before he slowed me down, pointing out that I'd used some of those combinations of cards several times. It was disappointing – and embarrassing - to learn that six of clubs, five of hearts and four of spades was exactly the same thing as four of spades, five of hearts and six of clubs, and any way you looked at them, it still counted as only fifteen two!

Bill and I fought a number of contests, as early adolescent boys are wont to do, but none peaked our passion as much as just after we read about the "Muggins" rule. Under the Muggins rule, you can take any points your opponent missed while counting his hand. In hind sight, it made us a lot more careful in counting our hands, but, believe me, it sparked an equal lot of anguish!

On our tour upstairs, I neglected to talk about the attic. Like most, it was cluttered, though only with the debris of a couple of generations, as the 1910 fire had taken out anything from earlier ancestors. You got to the attic via the long hallway in the upstairs apartment. There was a pull-down stairway, where you pulled on a sash cord, then released the stairs and down they came, sort of like an extension ladder. In fact, they came down with a vengeance if you weren't careful. The whole door mechanism was gently balanced; in the closed position it took only a gentle pull on the cord to lower the door to reach the ladder.

The attic was a regular treasure trove for us inquisitive youngsters. The largest feature in the attic was a huge copper-lined tank of water, poised somewhere about over the upstairs living room, next to the chimney. The tank was fed by the lead pipe water line from the spring up in the pasture near the blueberry patch. A float valve shut off the feed. Both the domestic cold water and the hot water, via that wood-burning heater in the Back Room, came from this tank.

In the main part of the attic there was an eclectic assortment of stuff. Here was a dress-maker's dummy, looking much the shape of Grammie Townsley. Carefully hidden away in a corner were what I assumed to be Uncle Floyd's war relics, the highlight of which was a Nazi sword or bayonet. It disappeared soon after I found it, and I never saw nor heard of it again.

And there in a box were Mother's old college biology texts.

Now, as farm kids, we were savvy about where babies come from, calves and kittens and puppies at least. Well, for the cows, though, it was confusing because we had Bill Fitzgerald, the artificial inseminator, pay a visit, but we watched the cats and dogs go at, so we kind of got the idea. By the time we were twelve or so, we'd had The Talk, and had learned with intended fear the horror of what happens when you put *that thing* in *that place*.

We knew, just from the way our parents mumbled and got red-faced and looked away, that sex must be a terrible thing. It didn't make sense, because the cats and dogs, and even those silly cows, acted like they might be enjoying it!

Mother's biology textbooks explained where the egg and the sperm came from and how they got together and what happened next. It was all pretty logical and straight forward. All that goofiness around The Talk! If they just explained it the way the texts did, it would have been so less stressful. So, as a twelve-year-old, you write that off as just one more thing that's going to be screwy in the adult world. And, boy, were we ever right!

My first experience hunting mice involved the attic. Like most farm houses, we sometimes had mice. You could hear them skittering in the ceilings and in the walls. Mother and Pres decided that a great way to get those pesky mice was to put Peter, our big yellow cat (you remember him, the fishnapper), upstairs in the attic. So one night, Peter was dispatched to the attic and the pull-down stairs were carefully raised, so as not to crush the tawny hunter.

During the night, Peter started prowling, and somewhere in the wee hours of darkness, he stalked across the business end of the pull down stairs. Much to his surprise – and everybody else's – the door dropped open, the stairs came crashing down, the cat squalled, Mother shrieked, and from my end of the house it sounded like one of the Orson Welles spooky stories I'd just heard on the radio that evening. Mother tore to the door of her bedroom and she said poor Peter was standing there shakily, his eyeballs appeared to be looking in different directions, and his ears didn't know whether to slink back in anger or prick up seeking her help.

After that Mother bought some old-fashioned Victor mousetraps and showed me how to bait them with peanut butter and set them. Over the next few days, I sent several mice off to meet their maker.

Pres and Ralph were apt to take a different approach. They thought D-Con was the far better answer. Mice and rats love the stuff. Laced with coumadin, an anti-coagulant, the vermin begin to bleed internally and soon die. In a barn that's not a bad thing because the barn smells mask the smell of a decaying mouse (or worse, rat!). In a house that's not nearly as welcome.

A dead mouse can linger - in essence, very literally - for weeks closed up in a wall.

There was a full cellar beneath the house, too. We'll talk about that later as we fill it with produce and firewood in the Fall for the Winter and Spring.

Chapter 2
Townsley Farm
The Barn and Outbuildings

Certainly the Townsley farmhouse, gleaming white, captures your attention as you approach the farm from the south. But it's the barn, applehouse and the other outbuildings where the farm is focused, where the main jobs of farming take place.

Townsley Farm, about 1953. Visible, left to right, the Bull Pen, Corn Crib, Barn, "Old" Silo, Farmhouse. The top of the second silo is visible to the left of the top of the old silo, and a corner of the Applehouse can be seen at to the right of the old silo. The hill at the left is Pumpkin Hill. In the distance between the house and the old silo is Roundtop.!
Dorothy N. Townsley Photo, Author's collection.

A definition may be in order before we proceed. Many farms today have an adjective associated with them: it's a dairy farm; it's an apple farm; it's a vegetable farm, and so forth. None of the farms in Apple Valley in the 1940s and 1950s could be identified to one principle line of business. Most Ashfield farms were barely more than subsistence farms, growing and raising enough to feed their family and, with luck, a little extra to sell or barter. Indeed, it's said that the truest definition of a farmer is a person who does whatever it takes to make a living. And all the Apple Valley farmers did whatever it took to make a living. The collection of buildings that made up the Townsley farm reflected that definition.

The applehouse, like all the buildings on the farm, was slate-roofed and painted red with white trim. It sat behind the farmhouse from the road, about on a level with the main entrance to the barn.

The applehouse had two levels. Two walls of the lower level were its fieldstone foundation. One of the rocks in the foundation has a picture of a horse carved there by neighbor Charlie Nadeau.

On the lower level, in season, was the apple-processing area. Before neighbor Richard Clark's storage was built, it was here that we sorted and packed the freshly picked apples for shipment to the wholesaler. Pres backed the loaded apple wagon into the lower level and unloaded the apples in their bushel boxes (the ones we kids had assembled during the summer) until they could be sorted and packed.

We had a sorting and grading crew that often included Mother and Dot Roberts and others. Gramp Nelson sometimes worked here and Jean Clark filled in occasionally when she wasn't picking. I helped pack apples after school and weekends when I wasn't picking.

The apples were sorted by variety, size, color and physical condition. Sorting and grading was tedious work. Sorters were on their feet all day and the apples were cold, as was the weather later in the season. Gloves didn't help, as they were slippery. It wasn't Mother's favorite job, but she soldiered on.

Apples were sorted and placed gently into bushel boxes that were lined with purple crepe paper. I've never figured out what purpose that purple paper served, but every box had to have a purple liner. As the bushel box was filled, it was pushed onto a conveyor that led to the final boxing step.

First of the final step in boxing the apples for shipping was to gently level off the box, that is, adjust the apples in the box so the box was full but not so overflowing that it couldn't be capped. Then a padded top was placed over the box, and the box was shaken to seat the apples in the box.

"Shaking them down" was another step that I have yet to understand. We had been taught, at every step from picking on down, that the apples had to be handled very carefully so as not to bruise them. Why on earth did we now, at the final stage of packing, purposely bruise them just before putting a cap on them!!?

The next step was to fold the ends of the purple paper over the top of the apples, position a 12 ½" x 16 ½" corrugated cardboard pad atop the paper, and nail two inch-wide slats to hold the cardboard in place. Capped boxes were stacked atop one another near the door in the corner of the applehouse nearest the milk room.

Once a week or so, a tractor-trailer rig with a forty- to forty-eight-foot box trailer would be backed up to the door (or as near as the driver could get). We moved the conveyor track so it could reach from the door to the inside of the trailer, and so loaded the trailer, keeping careful tally of the number boxes by variety, size, color and condition.

Off-season, the lower level of the applehouse served as a storage area. Much of the haying equipment was stored here, for example. Its comparatively low ceiling limited it to being a garage for nothing larger than the Farmall H tractor. In fact, you had to bend low as you drove it out of the applehouse. You could sit upright as you drove the smaller John Deere

Upstairs in the applehouse was the farm's machine shop. A pair of sliding doors opened between two butternut trees to look westward toward the apple orchards and beyond. I built a treehouse of sorts in the branches of the butternut that spread over the road to the orchard. It was just three or four planks laid over two horizontal branches, and it swayed gently when the wind blew. It was so cool to sit up there, hidden in the leaves, watching what went on beneath me.

Ralph spent a lot of his time upstairs in the applehouse, for this was a part of farming he liked most. He was adept at fixing and repairing machinery. He was an excellent welder, and had extensive equipment with which to ply this trade. He was especially good at cobbling up a tool or piece of equipment for use on the farm.

There were vices and grinders that were especially useful for sharpening the blades of the sickle bar mowing machine, for example. This was a special treat for a youngster to watch Ralph or Pres turn on the grinder and sharpen the triangular blades. It was exciting and pretty, in a Fourth-of-July way, to see the sparks fly off as the blade is touched to the grinding wheel.

There also was a big, old-fashioned grinding wheel that was powered by a foot pedal. It was used to sharpen scythes, mostly, so it didn't get much use, except by Pres. He was the last, as far as I know, to regularly use a scythe - to mow under the apple trees in the orchard.

Overhead on each side was where we stored the apple-picking equipment – the picking sacks, among other things. Over in back we stored the wood-cutting tools and equipment – axes, saws, wedges, chain-saw gas and oil and such.

The slate-roofed red barn was the largest structure on the farm. Typical of the valley farms, it had three levels, a manure pit underneath, the main floor where the livestock was kept, and the large hay loft at the top.

The manure pit was dark, dank and smelly, even by country standards. Although it was cleaned out at least once a year, there were usually several cone-shaped piles of cow and horse manure, one under each scuttle. In parts of the manure pit, under the horses, for example, the ceiling dripped horse urine and elsewhere cattle urine. Nothing lived in the manure pit except spiders, flies and the wilier rats and mice that had escaped the cats.

With the advent of the pole barn in 1958, the cows were moved outside year round, and the manure pit became a little more pleasant. Later in the 1960s, Townsleys housed their pigs there, and my kids, Robyn and Don, played with cousin Raymond and the pigs for hours.

The main floor of the barn is far more pleasant. In the early 1950s there were fifteen or so Holstein milking cows, about as many calves and young heifers, two Belgian work horses and a dozen cats and kittens.

Charlie Groff remembered, "Our cows were [then] all Ayrshires. They were serviced by an Ayrshire bull with tremendous horns. He weighed 2,300 pounds. This bull was so aggressive that Ralph would use a snap on staff attached to the ring in the bull's nose when leading the bull into the barnyard for serving. Ralph in addition carried a three foot long solid iron bar in one hand and a loaded .45 caliber revolver strapped to his hip."

One day when Charlie was ten, he was home with Grammie while all the other farm hands were off cutting logs and cordwood. "The bull got loose and wandered down Apple Valley Road. I went to the barn, put a halter on a cow and led the cow down the road to where the bull was.

"The bull followed the cow into the barn and luckily, he went into his pen and I locked him in," Charlie reports.

Grammie Townsley, sitting in her Morris chair, witnessed a parade we can only imagine: skinny, ten-year-old Charlie, nervously glancing back at the procession, followed by the cow on the leash, then the immense bull, and probably Scarlet, the border collie. She fainted.

Charlie continued, "I found Mother T. passed out on the floor of the dining room when I returned to the house."

The lower, older, silo was erected in the mid-1940s. I barely remember the men working on it as I looked on, barely more than a toddler, perched in a window in the upstairs porch over the milk room.

The upper silo was built about 1951, perhaps 1952. It was a little smaller than the older predecessor, both in height and diameter. Ralph tried to kill me while he was building this one. He was up on top of the space between the silo and the barn, working to add a roof, maybe. I came wandering through the entrance, which, like the entrance to the old silo, was from behind the horse stalls. Just as I came through the doorway, Ralph, twenty feet above, dropped his hammer. It crashed with a thump beside my left foot. It scared the tar out of both of us!

From the farmhouse porch, looking west, 1953. "New" silo at left, calving pen just beyond it. Corner of the corn crib behind it. Through the Notch are the apple orchard, Trefoil Piece and Charlie Tatro's over the top. The applehouse is at the right. My treehouse is in the butternut. Bruce, our pet Cocker Spaniel, was probably the subject of Mother's photo.
Dorothy N. Townsley Photo, Author's collection.

To the right of the main doors to the barn, about where the milking parlor is today, was a calving pen. Its back wall and end were made of big field stones, and it opened under the ramp to the hay loft toward the south. The side facing the new silo and the farmhouse beyond was, during the summer at least, made with planks spaced a foot or so apart.

I discovered first hand one day that there was barely enough room for a ten-year-old body between the boards when I squeezed in to admire a newly born calf. Unfortunately its Mama decided she didn't want any ten-year-old bodies visiting her new creation. She charged at me and butted my butt more times than I care to remember. I literally couldn't squeeze out of there quick enough - I'd just get one piece of my anatomy through the crack in the boards when she'd give me another push. It's a wonder I didn't break a bone or something.

Two machine sheds guarded the west-facing backside of the barn. One was directly over the small pen in which I was attacked by the cow. The other was right beside it. Both slate-roofed sheds were mainly for storing machinery and equipment. Shirley remembers there being a McClellan saddle stored in one of the two sheds, and she sometimes climbed onto it, dreaming of riding across the open range. I remember the sheds as just two more places where there were apt to be wasps and hornets.

The corn crib was an element of the past. A small building, more a shed than anything else, the corn crib was originally built to store husked ears of corn to be fed to the cattle. Our corn crib was perhaps eight feet wide by ten feet long. It was built a couple of feet or more off the ground to try to deter rats and other vermin. The most unique feature of a corn crib is that its walls are slats, so spaced that air can flow through more or less freely and dry the ears.

By my time, the corn crib was relegated to storing lumber and housing hornets. Its very openness and airiness was ideal to both tasks. We kids didn't spend much time there.

Filling the corn crib gave rise to an old farm custom, the Husking Bee. A season-ending harvest celebration, a husking bee drew all the neighbors to the host farm for the purpose of husking the thousands of ears of field corn. An incentive was offered: any young man who found an ear of red, Indian corn could kiss the any young woman he chose[4]. Frequently there was a good supply of liquor. If the host was really lucky, there was a musician or two among his friends. An evening of high hilarity ensued.

The only husking bee I can recall was at Charlie Nadeau's one fall evening. Three of us, Russ Williams, Craig Tanner and I, all about six or seven, maybe younger, scurried all over the pile, peeling back enough leaves of the husks to find a bunch of red ears. We were sternly told (by Francis Williams, I believe) to behave ourselves. Others had fun, but for the three of us the evening was pretty dull from that point on.

An aspect of growing up in Apple Valley was that we youngsters knew we were obliged to take direction – and punishment – and encouragement – from the neighbors as well as our own family. And it was equally assuring to know that if the Game Warden caught me hunting without a license, that I could be Bob Clark or Bob Williams or Bob Scott – and whoever's land I was hunting on (you could hunt legally on your own land without a hunting license) would swear to it! That comfort level was quickly erased when it dawned on me that Game Warden Albert Farrell knew exactly who I was,

---

4 One wag reported, "The gals were about as scarce as the red ears."

especially after the Beaver Dam Incident. We'll cover that item later, in the chapter on Spring.

Another shed called the bull pen stood behind the barn. Though it was tin-roofed, the bull pen was little more than a frame with a roof. The north side was boarded to provide some protection from the wind. There was a steel cable strung between the bull pen and the side of the barn. When Townsleys kept a bull, he could be chained, via the ring in his nose, to the cable, and thus given some freedom to move around, and some protection from the elements via the roofed pen. By my time, the east and south side were planked enough to keep the cattle out of it. The west end was open so that wagons or machinery could be stored under cover.

The bull pen was struck by lightning one evening during chores. The lightning bolt struck one of the rafters and split off a two foot long splinter

View looking back at the farm outbuildings, about November 1954. Pres is headed for the applehouse. The team, with Shirley up, is hitched to the stone cart in front of the woodshed. Behind the woodshed is the icehouse, converted by now into a shed where we assembled apple boxes. The barn with the two machine sheds, the corn crib and the applehouse are in the middle distance.
Author's Photo.

which shot like an arrow into a nearby wall. The bolt followed the cable into the barn, causing lots of sparks and excitement but no other damage.

I had finished my chores by then and was back in the house getting ready to do some homework. I felt my way along the pitch-black wall of my bedroom, feeling for my wall lamp. Just as I touched its switch, the lightning bolt hit with its instantaneous crack of thunder, and my first impression was that I had caused it by turning on the switch! Scared me 'most to death!

The main buildings at the farm (house, barn and applehouse) were protected by lightning rods. The idea behind lightning rods is to provide a path for lightning to follow when it strikes. I used to think that was a cool idea until the bull pen was struck: the lightning struck the far shorter bull pen, completely avoiding the three lightning rods on the nearby barn. But, in the larger picture, the barn was *not* hit, so the lightning rods *must* have worked! Maybe there's logic there…

Next beyond the bull pen, perhaps fifty yards or so, sat the icehouse. An important structure before refrigerators, it had fallen to disuse by the late 1940s. In its day, blocks of ice, destined for the farm's iceboxes, were stored here. The structure had sturdy thick walls and a well ventilated top. The ice blocks were stacked inside and covered with lots of sawdust as an insulator. On a hot summer day it was fun to scurry inside, scrape away the sawdust and chip off a little piece of ice to suck on. It didn't beat popsicles, but it was nice!

My only memory of World War II is tied to the icehouse. It was probably VE Day (May 8), the day the war ended in Europe. It may have been VJ Day (August 14) - it's more an impression than a memory - I was not yet five. I went with Gramp Nelson to get some ice from the icehouse. I heard cars honking in the distance as they drove up Ashfield Mountain. Gramp explained to me it probably was the end of the war.

About 1950, the icehouse was opened up and used as a shed. It was here that I earned my first wages by nailing boxes – assembling wooden apple crates. More about that later.

Six or eight feet west of the icehouse was the woodshed. A densely briar-filled alley separated the two structures. It was here that firewood for the wood stoves and the furnace in the house was worked up. Piles of odd logs, tree branches, pruned apple tree limbs and such were loosely stacked outside the woodshed. Periodically we mounted a saw rig to a tractor and cut the wood to the right length – eighteen inches or so – to fit in the stove or furnace.

The saw rig was a home made device, something OSHA would love today! Basically it featured a thirty inch diameter circular blade that was belt-driven from tractor. You wrestled the log to be cut onto a moveable table, then leaned the table into the screaming blade to cut off the desired length. The blade was completely unprotected, chips and splinters of wood could fly off in any direction, and the constant whine of the saw was literally deafening.

Nonetheless, we soldiered on; it was a job that had to be done, and despite the lack of any protective gear we lived through it.

The wood-hauling cart, about 1952. Bill Townsley is on the driver's seat beside Uncle Pres, behind him are his sisters Ginny and Lynn. Shirley Townsley and Bob Bates are standing.
Dorothy N. Townsley photo, Author's Collection.

From time to time, in between other jobs, we were assigned to split wood, that is, break it into smaller pieces to fit in the stove or furnace. I hated it at the time. It was strenuous, boring work. Again, age changes one's perspective. I find it now to be settling, a way to release some frustrations and get a little exercise along the way. It's still strenuous and boring!

Finally, the wood had to be carted from the woodshed to the house where it would be consumed. Pres used a heavy, fifth-wheel cart, drawn by his team of horses, for this purpose. The cart had been designed to carry rocks and stumps and such, from newly cleared (or recently plowed) fields, so it was sturdy! You could put a small load of wood in it ("'bout a thimble-full," somebody once sneered) to haul it to the house.

We had a chute that would fit in one of the cellar windows. It was a heavy oak affair, with three steel bars, a couple of inches wide, a quarter inch thick and perhaps a couple of feet long, affixed to the throat to help the sticks slide through the window. That enabled us to toss the wood sticks in the general area and they'd tumble through the window onto the cellar floor below. Every fourth or fifth load, one of us, usually me, ducked into the cellar to clear the accumulated wood away from the window to make room for some more.

It was one such occasion that I first drove the team.. Pres suggested I drive the team back to the woodshed while he stepped into the house for something.

Now, keep in mind, Pres was not an especially great teacher. He believed in the principle that if your student watches carefully, he'll soak up all he (or she) needs to master the task. In some situations this may actually work, but only if the student knows he's supposed to be a student, and if the student actually watches carefully. This student was aware neither that he was a student, nor that he was supposed to be watching, and so was nearly clueless when he gingerly sat on the seat and picked up the reins.

The team, being creatures of habit, understood when they felt the reins being picked up, that they were to move forward. And, as they had been doing all day, they were to turn to the left, between the buildings and on toward the woodshed.

It was so cool! I was actually *driving* the team! Up through the farm yard we went, and I was *driving the team*!!! The team swung in toward the woodshed, then turned slightly to the right toward the sugarhouse – and stopped.

It began to dawn on me in the silence and the breeze that all I had done was to hold the reins for the last five minutes or so. Now I had to back this big stubby cart into the woodshed. And in this moment of awakening, I couldn't remember "Gee" from "Haw!" Even the meaning of "Whoa" was becoming unclear!

There was another insidiously hidden factor to which I hadn't yet connected. This was a fifth-wheel cart – its "fifth wheel" referring to it being jointed in the middle. It means even experienced drivers sometimes get in trouble when they try to back a trailer.

Well, Pres always said something like, "Back!" at this point, and pulls back on the reins.

I tried, "B-back!" and pulled on both reins. The horses started to back – and that fifth wheel cart quickly started to fold in the middle!

"Um- Ah- STOP!" I shouted, but that meant nothing to the team, and they kept on backing.

In desperation, I swung the free end of the reins and whacked the near horse on the rump. She stopped for a second, then, confused, lunged forward. The off horse hadn't got the message and continued back for moment before he decided he's better go along forward with his teammate. Finally, "Whoa!" came to mind, and in a swirl of motion and flying snow we came to a stop.

I glanced around to see if Pres was coming, but he was nowhere in sight. He hadn't seen that moment of stellar driving, and I might yet have time to figure it out. I looked around. The team was pointed northwest toward the sugarhouse. The back part of the cart was pointed east, toward the icehouse. The horses looked at each other nervously.

I tried, "Back" again, but when I saw immediately that was to be a disaster, I hollered, "WHOA! Whoa! Whoa." The team had lurched back, then stopped in a stomping clumsy way. Even in the cold, there was sweat building under their collars and flecks of spittle at the corners of their mouths. Maybe mine, too.

It came to mind about now that Pres might have used Gee or Haw in situations like this. Which one means Go Left and which means Go Right?

When the snow had settled and the horses were breathing easier, I tried, "haw." Nothing happened, and I concluded I might have said it pretty softly. "Haw!" I tried again, trying to sound as if I actually knew what I meant.

After a moment the horses started to step sideways to the left! Way cool! Haw is Left! The team kept sidestepping. Now they're aimed toward the ice pond, and they're still side-stepping. Now they're pointed into the woodshed. "Yikes!" I shouted, but that wasn't the magic word. Finally "Whoa!" came to mind. Again, this time in a swirl of sawdust, wood litter and dust, we came to a halt.

The business end of the cart was still pointed back in the direction of the farmhouse, but the team had now traveled about a half mile going backwards and forwards and sideways. About this point Pres rounded the corner, a welcome relief for me, but the team was even happier to see him than I was!

He glanced at me wordlessly, but there was just the hint of a grin as he climbed onto the driver's seat and took the reins. I think he knew, from the frothing team and my glazed eyes, about what had transpired, and he never said a word about it to me.

I never drove the team again until many years later.

There is a "rest of the story" to this "first time" tale. I became adept at backing fifth wheel rigs with a tractor or a truck before long, and eventually was able to apply the principles of backing with a motor vehicle to driving equines. The magic was patience, confidence and complete commands.

A few years later, I drove a team on my summer job at Naushon Island to meet an arriving VIP, and swung the team in a tight circle at the dock. In five short commands, I backed the carriage under the overhang and out of the rain:

"Whoa," and pulling gently back on the reins to stop their forward motion.

"Gee," to sidestep them to the right.

"Whoa," to stop them from sidestepping.

"Back," then "Haw," to back them while stepping to the left.

"Whoa," to stop them – precisely where I had wanted to!

Pres wasn't there to appreciate my triumph, nor was Pete Bundy, my immediate boss. I knew, and that was enough.

The farthest building toward the west, right along the little brook that comes out of the orchard, was the sugarhouse. Most of the year it sat idle.

The apple picking ladders were stored up overhead, and we'd haul them out in the late summer and hopefully put them away again before snow flew. Other than during the late winter and early spring, the only time we approached it was to replenish the supply of wood slabs that Fred would use for fire during the maple season. We'll visit the sugarhouse later in Winter.

Perhaps the most photographed building on the farm was the automobile garage across the road from the farmhouse. It shows up in almost every picture of visitors, or big loads of logs, or monstrous wagon-loads of hay, or a hazy morning sunrise down the valley. Like many other farm buildings, it was slate-roofed and painted red with white trim. It was built as a two-car garage, but it was nearly long enough to house four cars if they were the dimensions of vehicles of the teens and twenties.

Fred's and Preston's cars were parked here. Fred owned a Packard in the mid to late 1940s; he was pretty proud of it. Pres owned a succession of cars, all of them previously owned. The first I remember is a brown and cream Chevrolet sedan, perhaps a 1949 model. When the '49 Chevy bit the dust about 1952, it was followed by a black 1950 Chevy with an automatic transmission. Man, I thought that was just about perfection. It was just what I wanted when I got my license and could buy my own car.

One summer evening Pres drove Bill Townsley and me in that black Chevy up to Harry Jerome's for haircuts. Harry worked in Greenfield, I think, and cut hair on the side to help make ends meet. As we drove back up through the valley, all three of us across the front bench seat, Bill, in the

The oft-photographed garage, 1940 or before. The butcher shop has not yet been built. Clark's east orchard begins atop the hill and off to the right. Apple Valley Road is just the far side of the mailbox.
Unknown photographer, Author's Collection.

middle, gave me a glance and a gentle elbow in the ribs, and exclaimed, "Wow, did you see that?"

As he did, Bill gestured off through the windshield at whatever imagined thing it might be, and neatly nudged the column-mounted gear-shift lever from Drive to Neutral. As Pres, startled, peered to see what he missed, the car began to slow and the motor to whine. His immediate panic was that something ailed the car, and he steered to the side and gunned the engine a couple of times. Then he discovered what had happened, and soon had a pretty good idea how it happened. I don't think Pres ever fully forgave Bill for that episode.

Pres had a series of Pontiacs, beginning with a 1954 Chief, after that Chevy. He relied on Alfred Nadeau, who then worked at Don Lorenz, the Greenfield Pontiac dealer, to pick him out a good used car, and Alfred never failed him.

Now, half a century later, I wonder why the garage was the only building at the time that was built a hundred yards or more across the road from the nearest farm building. Did Fred not trust those new-fangled automobiles? His early cars pre-dated any other internal combustion contrivance by twenty years or more. Hmmm…

Between the garage and the brook was the Butcher Shop. It was constructed in the mid-1940s, one of few buildings on the farm not to have a slate roof. It was large enough, and had wide-enough sliding doors, that Ralph could race a truck loaded with hay bales into it as the first drops from an approaching thunderstorm began to fly. In the winter and spring, however, it was used for its primary purpose, a butcher shop.

One morning very soon after it was built, Fred walked through the yard, headed from the applehouse toward the new butcher shop. Then yet an inquisitive toddler of four or so, I hollered, "Where you going?"

"Bughouse!" he replied.

Moments later when Pres asked where Fred went, I duly reported, "He went Bughouse." Ever after, the butcher shop was "Bughouse." To everyone except Ralph.

Today, friends who weren't raised on a farm ask in shock, "Didn't it bother you to kill animals as a youngster?" Most are shocked even more when I reply, "Yes, there's always at least a twinge. But you do what you must, and you get on with it."

Farmers kill for several reasons. One is to protect your family, your farm, your livestock and your fields from vermin and other marauders. A second reason is to feed your family and others. A third reason is for sport, as a fisherman and hunter. And another reason you kill is to euthanize sick or injured animals. For a farmer, a gun is just another farm tool.

The first reason needs little explanation. It's why Gramp Nelson shot the fox in the meadow where his pullets ranged. It explains trapping – or poisoning - mice and rats. It explains, in part, at least, my hunting for woodchucks, though there's an element of sport in woodchucking.

The necessity for killing to feed yourself and your family is also reasonably obvious. We are a society of omnivores, and much of our diet comes from our gardens – and from the very animals we raise.

There's little doubt that more farmers are hunters and fishermen than of most other vocational groups. There is an element of "feeding the family" here, but we no longer need to hunt wild animals to feed our loved ones.

It's that fourth reason for killing that causes farmers the most stress and sleepless nights, but like it or not, euthanasia is part of your responsibility as a custodian of animals.

As a farmer, you take ample steps to assure that your livestock remains healthy, that your pets are thoroughly and timely vaccinated against rabies and distemper and the like. Indeed, Dr. Streeter, the local veterinarian, was a regular visitor at Townsley Farm.

However, part of that responsibility in caring for your animals is ending your animals' misery. That last part requires you to euthanize your hopelessly sick or injured animals. It's a part you truly agonize over. It's even worse when that animal is a treasured and trusted pet, as in "Old Yeller". But in the end, it is another of your responsibilities.

Chapter 3
The Neighborhood

Driving into Apple Valley from Route 112 for the first time in the mid-1950s, it appeared that you were headed into a deep and dark wilderness. The trees along the road guarded the pavement and blocked out the sun. Beside the road were two dramatic waterfalls. Presently, as you came around Piano Corner (more about that in a few pages), the valley began to open up with fields and orchards.

For much of the twentieth century the first farm you came to as you drove into Apple Valley was Nelson's. Here lived my mother's parents, "Gramp" and "Nannie" Nelson to most of the kids in the lower valley.

A dramatic and picturesque waterfall in the lower valley.
Donald N. Bates Photograph.

I had spent much of my infancy in Nannie's care as Mother went to her parents' home to grieve over my Dad's death, first in Norwell, then later at the new farm in Apple Valley. As our nearest neighbor, Nannie and Gramp were huge influences over Shirley and me.

Shirley or I often spent nights at Nannie and Gramp's, and it was always something we welcomed. I almost always slept in "the pink room," one of several upstairs bedrooms. I would drift off to sleep to the murmur of the radio from downstairs as Gramp and Nannie listened to "One Man's Family." After it was over, Gramp would read aloud from the Bible. A leaky faucet in the sink in the nearby bathroom lullabied, "plink, plink, plink," as I slipped off to sleep.

We youngsters often slipped into bed with Nannie and Gramp at sunrise the next morning, and I remember the musty slept-in smell of the bedclothes. On cold mornings we'd skitter downstairs and dress behind the stove in the kitchen. I remember rainy mornings and the smell of Gramp's rain gear, wet from doing chores before breakfast.

Nannie Nelson was innately a positive reinforcer. When you talked to her, she always (as nearly as I can remember, anyway) put aside what she was doing and gave you her full attention. That was heady stuff for a ten-year-old. Though we couldn't have told you why then, its obvious now why her grandchildren liked to visit: they were always welcomed and treated as adults.

But it was more than that. Nannie often baked an angel food cake with frosting as a birthday cake for the appropriate youngster. Walnut crèmes, but preferably without the walnuts, was a favorite treat. So was ginger bread with egg sauce and the once a year treat, strawberries still cool from the strawberry patch, hulled, then rolled in sugar! Nannie not only spoiled us with goodies, but she wielded a mighty needle and thread as she made clothes for most of her grandchildren.

Gramp Nelson would take me as a youngster with him while he worked in the woods, getting out stove and chunk wood[5] for heating. I don't think he ever sold wood. We'd go up towards the Picnic Place in his old blue 1928 Ford van. He always made me feel that I was helping, though I expect I was a pain in the neck, as most six year olds can be. It was all hand work, hand saws, axes and wedges. I also "helped" Gramp build the brooder house[6] that Steve Greenman tore down in 1994 to make room for his garage. I worked

---

5 "Getting out wood" is the process of cutting trees down and preparing wood for burning in stoves (for cooking) and furnaces (for heat). Stoves required finer stock, 15 inches or so long and as big around as one's forearm, but furnaces could take larger "chunks".

6 A brooder house is specially equipped building where you put a new brood of baby chicks. Gramp Nelson had several; "the slaughterhouse" was one. He got his baby chicks from Avery's hatchery in Colrain.

for what seemed to be a week pounding one nail into a board on the backside of the building.

Gramp always said grace before meals, and I'd give a good deal more than a nickel to know what the words were. All I can remember is that we gave thanks "for earthly bounty," but that's the only snippet I can summon.

Gramp Nelson made me a little table; it's now under the model railroad downstairs in my cellar in Nashua. There's also a WWII wooden cartridge box down there that held a tool set he gave me as a youngster; it may be worth more than all the tools it once held. There's a desk under my cellar stairs that was made by Rev. Eleazer Farr, MD, perhaps in the 1880s. An ordained Baptist minister and a practicing physician, Farr was Gramp Nelson's grandfather, which makes him my great-great grandfather.

Nannie and Gramp were regular church-goers and joined the Ashfield Congregational Church immediately after their move to Apple Valley. Gramp became a Deacon, and Nannie was a leader in the Ladies Circle. Neither Gramp nor Nannie ever swore - I certainly never heard either swear, though Gramp Nelson came very close one day as he was moving grain bags in his "milk room" and discovered grain pouring out through a huge hole the rats had chewed on their way in to feast.

During the summer we kids – Shirley and I, with whomever of the Greenman cousins was visiting - gravitated to the brook behind the house. We fished there and we built dams there.

Once I fashioned a boat using the slats that bound the shavings Gramp got for the chickens' litter. I proudly carted it to the brook and floated it in the water. But when I stepped into it the first time, I was astonished when the water gushed in. My poor boat barely slowed my descent to the bottom of the tiny pool.

When it was REALLY hot, Nannie would bring out a big washtub on the lawn in front of her kitchen and fill it with water from the garden hose. It was incredibly cold at first, but the sun soon warmed it up. We didn't need our bathing suits - we would jump in wearing just our underwear.

It was always pleasant to visit Gramp and Nannie, and Shirley and I visited often. It was a place to go when we were frustrated or felt picked on or thought life was being unfair. And it was a place to proudly announce our achievements and triumphs. I know now that not everyone has a Gramp and Nannie of the stature of Shirley's and mine. How sad.

Continuing northwesterly up Apple Valley Road, you approach a bridge crossing Clessons Brook. The bridge was for many years tended by a large black cherry tree, and it provided a majestic frame for your introduction to the Townsley farm.

At the Townsley farmhouse lived Fred and Alta Townsley, downstairs; and Pres and Dot, Shirley and me lived upstairs. We visited here earlier.

Clif and Mildred Scott lived a little farther up the road and up the hill. They lived downstairs, and Bud and Bunny Scott and their family lived upstairs. Bud was Clif and Mildred's second son, after daughter Gladys and son Ed. Fred, the youngest son, married neighbor Lois Williams; he became a veterinarian with a practice near Cornell University. Clif had been the Agriculture teacher and baseball coach at Sanderson Academy for a while, and for most of the last of his life was an Ashfield selectman. Once in a while I helped Clif and Bud with chores.

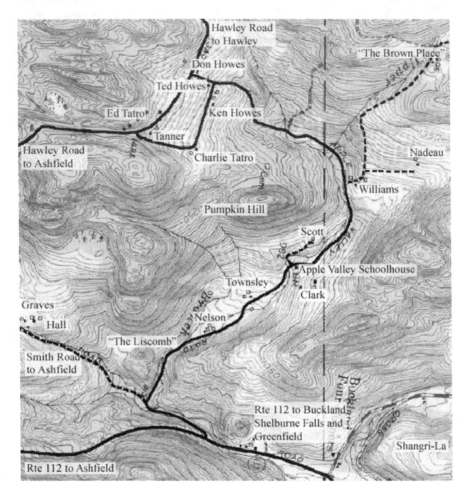

The Neighborhood
In the Mid 1950s

Apple Valley in the northwest part of Ashfield as it was in the mid-1950s, looking westerly from Ridge Hill. Scanned from Ashfield Quadrangle, 7.5 Minute Series, Rev 1955.
Map courtesy of the U.S. Geological Survey

The Scotts had a gutter cleaner[7] in their barn. I thought that mechanical wonder was the coolest thing ever until I found that you still had to apply a hoe or shovel here and there, and that the system was down for repairs from time to time.

Bud and Bunny built a sugar house at the foot of the hill. For years steam poured into the night as they boiled off the sap.

Turning right, just across a short bridge, was the Apple Valley Schoolhouse. Until about 1940 all the Valley children gathered here for lessons. It sat vacant for a few years until Martha and Ralph Townsley purchased it and remodeled it as a dwelling. Ralph and Martha lived here from their marriage in 1946 until The Great Townsley Shuffle in 1958[8].

Continuing past the old schoolhouse there was a pair of right turns, actually a loop, up to Malcolm and Pauline Clark's home, then looping up past the older family farm where three Clark generations then lived: "Gramma" Bertha Clark, her daughter-in-law, Ruth, and Ruth's bachelor son, Richard.

Malcolm and Pauline's cape featured a large picture window with a beautiful view down the valley past Townsley's and Nelson's, and to Ridge Hill in the distance. I babysat for them a number of times, and once I got Aaron, Brian and Dana to bed, it was time to gaze out that picture window. The summer sun had long since finished setting over Pumpkin Hill, and night crept stealthily out of the lower valley and the brook, chasing daylight up through Townsley's orchards.

I worked for Malcolm off and on in the early 1960s. One spring we spent time getting out firewood for heat for their home. One afternoon I was splitting some of the larger logs, swinging a good-sized maul and using a couple of steel wedges to work through some of the knotty poplars. I felt something strike the back of my mittened hand after a particularly lusty swing but barely gave it a thought. A few minutes later, my mitten felt damp, which was odd, because it wasn't especially warm, so it couldn't be sweat. I glanced down, and the gray mitten was dripping blood! Apparently a flake of steel had flown off the wedge and struck me between the first and second

---

7 The gutter gleaner was an electric motor driven conveyor of sorts. It lay in the gutter behind the cows. You opened the scuttles in the gutter then turned on the machine, and if it worked as planned, the conveyor swept the cow manure to the scuttles. In principle, at least, you never had to lift a shovel or hoe ever again! It was the envy of all the local farmers!

8 The Great Townsley Shuffle even made it into the *Greenfield Recorder-Gazette*. The Ralph Townsleys moved briefly into a trailer, the Preston Townsleys moved into the schoolhouse, Grammie Townsley moved upstairs at the farmhouse, and finally Ralph and his family moved into the farmhouse's downstairs apartment. The whole process took only three or four days.

knuckle, just missing the tendon on one side and barely nicking a large vein on the other side. It took several minutes to stop the bleeding. Eventually I was able to put a bandaide over the wound and it healed nicely. However, I still have a faint scar as a reminder.

Malcolm liked to take a break between whatever we were doing and evening chores. We'd head to his dining area with a pot of coffee, and there discuss events and whatever else needed talking about. I came to enjoy those moments of re-charge; I wasn't the hired man then, he made me feel that we were colleagues.

Malcolm's and Richard's mother, Ruth lived at the Clark farmhouse, along with her mother-in-law, Bertha. I barely knew Gramma Clark. She was unable to get around very well, and was profoundly deaf by the time I knew her during the last of her life in Apple Valley.

Ruth was very slight, but full of energy and good humor. She genuinely cared about her neighbors and fretted about their well-being. In fact, those neighbors chuckled that they didn't need to worry about anything – Ruth worried enough for everyone!

But Ruth's worrying about her neighbors typified the very best of Ashfield neighborliness. Her neighborliness often manifested itself in gifts of bread or pastries in times of trouble. Ruth's pastries were renowned in town. Her hot cross buns were legendary, light and fluffy and gently browned, with lots of raisins and a tasty frosting cross on their tops. Sadly, Ruth became increasingly blind, to the point where she could no longer make the delicious pastries. Everyone in the Valley mourned the passing of those heavenly rolls and hot cross buns!

Richard was a quiet, hard worker. He put in his time in the barn, doing milking chores and such, but, like Pres Townsley, his heart was in the orchard. Richard worked the Clark apple orchards mostly alone, or sometimes with the help of Buckland neighbor, Raymond "Bump" Valiton. Richard claimed to have been struck by lightning several times. I wouldn't doubt it; he was tough and wily enough to face God down with the comment, "Not now. Got work to do!"

Richard had a big red hound named Peter, and he chided Wayne Jones and me that Peter got twice as many woodchucks as we did.

A third sibling of Richard and Malcolm Clark was Barbara Graves. She and husband Arthur visited from time to time, but her daughter, Pat, visited often during the summers and was part of the haying crew. Pat was one of Shirley's heroes, slightly older, with a quick and down-to-earth sense of humor.

Apple Valley Road turns toward the north above Clarks, and crosses the town line from Ashfield into Buckland. Soon the substantial farmhouse, barn and outbuildings of Williams's appear to the right.

Lillian and Francis Williams, with their children, Connie and Russell, lived downstairs. Francis' brother, Harry, lived upstairs with his wife, Ethel, and daughter, Lois. I barely remember Rob and Winnie Williams, Harry and Francis' parents. Winnie died in the late 1940s, and Rob remarried and lived for several more years.

Russ Williams and I have been friends for as long as I remember. We often played together as youngsters. One afternoon at his house, he and I fashioned swords from the slats that bound the shavings Francis got for the chickens. His mom made us pirate hats from old newspapers. One thing led to another until, inevitably, we pirates got into a swordfight. I ended up with a pretty deep gash on my chin.

Russell's mom organized a Cub Scout den when Russ and I were of age. We met at Lillian's, where she had all sorts of fun projects for us to work on. We took some photographs one day; my first-ever photo was of Russell skiing down the slope from the Williams hayloft.

Russ Williams, skiing down the slope from Williams' hayloft, about 1951.
Author's photo.

Williams' pasture was across the road from the barn and behind the farmhouse. It had a little brook meandering through it that was ideal for making dams and stuff. He had lots of nice sloppy mud and sod, perfect for making some great dams that actually raised the level of the water behind them. One of his dams earned the ultimate compliment: a trout adopted the pool behind it as home! I envied Russell for his brook. The one in our pasture splashed and tumbled over the rocks down the edge of our pasture and wasn't very dam-able.

Russell contracted polio in 1952 but he never complained about it. From my vantage point he was pretty mobile. He and I still went fishing like before. Later, when we were old enough, he and I, along with his dog,

Freckles, went hunting rabbits in that same pasture. Russ could pole vault over the brush, while Freckles and I had to fight our way through it.

Harry and Francis made syrup for many years. One afternoon Lillian invited me up to join Russell for sugar-on-snow[9]. Lillian offered a plate of pickles. Russ took a big bite of one, and apparently it was much more sour than he expected. He soldiered on, however, and offered me one, saying through a grimace, "Hey, try one, Bob. They're... delicious!" Except that a shudder slipped in between "They're" and "delicious."

Ethel Williams, Russell's aunt, was our first grade teacher. Harry and Ethel's daughter, Lois, baby-sat for Shirley and me a couple of times. Neither she nor we appear to have been traumatized by that circumstance. Lois became the bride of neighbor Fred Scott.

Francis and Lillian Williams decided to sell the old family farm just up Apple Valley Road from us in 1962. Part of selling an old family farm was to empty out the farmhouse of at least three generations of household goods, and the traditional method of doing that was to hold an old-fashioned country auction.

One of the big items in the auction was the family's old player piano[10]. It was old and the tubing inside was brittle and broken, but with work, it could sing once more. Blanche Ward, a widow from up in Ashfield village, bid and won the ancient piano. She asked her boyfriend, Richard Clark, our neighbor just up the road from us, to move it for her from Williams's to her house in Ashfield.

One day, succumbing to pressure, Richard and Bump Valiton, his hired man, drove up to Williams's and backed Bump's pickup up to Francis and Lillian's front door. Richard and Bump really struggled to load the piano, which seemed to weigh a ton, into the back of the pickup.

"Don't suppose we ought to tie it down, do you, Bump?" Richard asked. Richard was a worrier.

"Naw! Hard's we worked to get that on, it ain't coming offa there," Bump assured, and off down through the valley the load went.

---

9 Sugar-on-Snow is a treat even for seasoned old Yankees. Charlie Groff reported, "Sugaring-off parties were held two or three times every winter. Enamel pans 18" across by 6" deep were filled with firmly compressed snow. Maple syrup was slowly boiled until it would form a soft ball when dropped into cold water. Then it was ready to drizzle over the snow's surface." Family and lucky neighbors could then pick the sticky stuff out the packed snow with a fork. Pickles were often served to accent and peak the intensely sweet taste of the "sugar".

10 The *Moving the Piano* story is pretty much as Bump Valiton told it to me soon after it happened about 1963.

Now Apple Valley necks down and gets pretty curvy along the banks of Clesson's Brook below Nelson's, and sure enough, at what is known today as Piano Corner, the piano rolled out of the back of the pickup and crashed down the bank, coming to rest at last in the brook.

Richard looked back just as the piano started to roll, and observed, "Oh Gawd, Bump, there it goes!"

Bump glanced back and agreed, "Yup, sure did."

The two intrepid movers stopped the truck and stood on the edge of road, trying to figure what to do next.

"What am I going to do?" fretted Richard. "What am I going to tell Blanche?"

They studied it a while. Finally Bump said, "OK. Get back into the truck. I'll handle everything."

Presently they arrived in Blanche's front yard. Blanche knew something was wrong. "Richard got out of the truck and just stood there, staring at his shoes and sort of pawing the dirt," she said.

Bump, true to his word, reached into the back of the pickup and offered, "Well Blanche, here's your piano stool. If you want the piano, it's back there in the brook."

Blanche and Richard were married not too long after that. They built the house where Roland Townsley and his family live now. Richard bought Blanche a splendid working player piano as a wedding gift.

Steve Greenman and other local fishermen said that every high water, as the sounding board contracted and expanded, the Williams's old piano would play a regular serenade. It lay in the brook bed (at Piano Corner) for years before it finally broke up.

Continuing up the hill through Harry and Francis's farmyard, the road straight ahead goes up through Williams' sugar orchard to "the Brown place."

Taking a right leads to Charlie and May Nadeau's farm. Charlie was a World War I veteran and had pretty much retired from farming when I knew him. Charlie and May had two sons, Alfred, an auto mechanic in Greenfield; Gordon, a farmer/rancher just outside Austin, Texas; and their developmentally challenged daughter, Jean, who lived with them in Apple Valley.

The view from Charlie and May's was spectacular. Their farm was uniquely set halfway up Apple Valley. Down the valley to the left, below Pumpkin Hill, you could see past Williams's to Scott's and Clark's, with Ridge Hill in the distance. Up the valley to your right and on the flanks of Pumpkin

Hill were Howes's and Tatro's. I always dreamed of living at Charlie's house someday, sometime later when I could afford it. I'm still waiting.

As a young man I enjoyed woodchucking in a couple of the fields behind and above Charlie Nadeau's. I don't remember slaying many woodchucks, but I treasured the visits with Charlie afterwards. Most often we sat smoking a cigarette while Charlie shared his experience working with Pres, whom he respected and loved; and Fred, whom he guardedly respected.

Charlie could get philosophical. One evening, as I complained about getting out stovewood, he said, "Think about how many times wood keeps you warm. It starts when you walk into the woods. You keep warm cutting the tree down and limbing it out [cutting the limbs off], cutting it to a rough length, loading the cut logs onto the logging sled, then unloading them again at the woodshed.

"Once at the woodshed, you keep warm cutting the logs into stovewood lengths, and Lord knows, you keep warm splitting wood. You keep warm loading it onto the cart, and again back at the house as you toss the cut wood into the cellar. You keep warm lugging it upstairs to the woodboxes. Finally you get to burn it! But wait, you're not done! You keep warm taking out and spreading the ashes!"

After Williams's, Apple Valley Road turns southwesterly, back into Ashfield and up the hill toward the upper valley. About halfway up the hill on the right was the small trailer of Cecil Bolton. I was never sure how the spell his nickname; it was pronounced as if it was spelled *CEASE*. Cecil worked for Ted Howes.

One day in the mid-1950s Cecil spotted a pheasant not far from his home. With visions of a tasty broiled pheasant on his platter, he ran to get his shotgun. Here's the story as I remember it. The shotgun was an ancient weapon, but he thought little of it as he loaded a very modern shotgun shell, drew a bead and fired. The barrel of the shotgun exploded under the pressure, taking much of Cecil's forearm with it. He sported a hook for the rest of his life. The shotgun was constructed of Damascus steel[11] which even then was considered unsafe, especially with today's high-powered smokeless powder shells. His hook served as a cautionary tale for all us young hunters.

Ted and Evelyn Howes and their three daughters, Carol, Sharon and Janice, lived just a little ways farther up the road. Ted and Evelyn were

---

11 "Damascus or twist-steel barrels are made by layering alternate strips of steel and iron then welding them together. ...one should never, ever consider shooting a Damascus, twist or laminated-steel barreled shotgun..." *-http://www.briley.com/articles/grampas_shotgun.html.*

contemporaries of Mother and Pres. Carol and Sharon were Shirley's and my ages. Janice was a bit younger.

Ted was the very image of a craggy slow-talking New Englander, especially as he grew older. Evelyn, my mom's closest friend in the Valley, was just the opposite, wise-cracking and fun-loving. The entire Valley was devastated at Evelyn's untimely death. She succumbed to cancer in the mid-1950s, leaving Ted and his daughters, the oldest of whom was then an early teenager.

A hundred yards farther up the hill, at the corner of Hawley Road, was Don Howes's. Don had several apple orchards nearby, and he processed his apples in the big white barn at the intersection. I remember Don's wife, Hortense, as a story-teller. One day at a church function, I think, she told the story of *Tikki tikki tembo-no sa rembo-chari bari ruchi-pip peri pembo*, to the ohs and ahs of us youngsters.

Taking the left at Ted and Evelyn's brought you into the Howes family farmyard. Gladys and Ken Howes lived here with their children, Joy Ann and Ronnie. Ron was about my age, Joy was a little older. Ken and Ted's mom, Jessie, lived at the farmhouse, too. She was a very old woman whom I barely knew, a contemporary of Grammie Townsley, Ruth Clark, Rob and Winnie Williams and Charlie and Lena Tatro. She passed away at about the horizon of my awareness, in the mid 1940s.

Ken Howes had a beautiful 1928 Chevy Coupe – with a rumble seat in the back. I hitched a ride home with Ken and Ron one afternoon after baseball practice, riding in the rumble seat. Talk about windblown!

Walking home to Townsley's from Howes's took me through Charlie and Lena Tatro's farm. They, too, were long retired by the time I became aware. Pres cut timber on several of Charlie's woodlots for a number of years.

At Tatro's the road bears to the right, and at its intersection with Hawley Road lived Guy and Kay Tanner and their son, Craig. Kay was one of Charlie and Lena's daughters. Craig was a classmate of Russ Williams and me.

Across Hawley Road from Tanner's was Ed and Dot Tatro's home. Their eldest, Jim, was several years younger than Russ Williams and me. He was always one of the bratty little kids that rode the school bus with us in the later 1950s.

The walk from Tatro's down to Townsley's was much easier than going the other way. You walked a short way up the hill through their pasture, being careful to close any gates or barways behind you. At the top of the pasture the view opened up, and you paused here for a moment in awe, drawing in the grandeur.

Your first impression was visual: you could see for miles to the north and northeast, past Putt's Hill and well into Shelburne.

Then you became aware of the quiet. How still it was! Yet as you stood there absorbing the moment, you became aware of the last of the day sounds – the crickets and robins with the breeze rattling the poplar leaves.

At twilight, the setting sun's rays fleetingly kissed the highest hills, then painted a distant thunderhead in shades of pink and gold. Deep in the dense and darkening woods a wood thrush performed its pan-pipe trill.

After a few moments, you stepped forward into the gathering dusk. A symphony of night sounds slowly swelled out of the woods just below and filled you with a sense of wonder and peace as you walked down the hill toward home.

Chapter 4
Memorial Day and Other Events

There was a special kind of magic about Memorial Day. Above all else, it was a day to pause and remember all those who gone before us. We focused especially on those who have fallen while defending our country. The day was especially meaningful to those whose sons, husbands, fathers and friends rode away from home, full of promise and confidence, never to return. The Townsley family was among them, having lost son and brother, Harold, over the Bay of Biscay in World War II. Memorial Day had a very tangible and tender poignancy to it that no other holiday had.

Ashfield celebrated Memorial Day on May 31 each year with a parade, school exercises[12] and recitations, a speech by a notable person, lunch at the Congregational Church, wrapping things up with a baseball game between the alumni and the current Sanderson Academy team.

In a larger sense, Memorial Day was a collective sigh of relief at having survived another winter. Of all the things we worried about last Fall, very few came to fruition. Of those problems that did arise, we either resolved or endured them. In the final analysis, we had made it to Memorial Day, so everything was going to be OK.

For Gramp Nelson, caretaker of the town's cemeteries for several years, preparing for Memorial Day involved making sure that the two larger cemeteries, the Plain Cemetery and Hill Cemetery, were manicured to the best of his ability. I was often asked to help out, at the princely wage of 75 cents an hour. It was the first job at which I actually got paid by the hour.

For Scoutmaster Merton Howes, it meant acquiring the right number of American flags, then overseeing the placement of the flags at the burial sites of those who served in the armed forces. We Boy Scouts, on the Saturday before Memorial Day, would fan out across the cemeteries trying to find all the

---

12 "Exercises" consisted of recitations, songs, poems and the like, performed by some or all the students in each of the upper grades and some of the high school groups. The exercises were presented at the Town Hall immediately after the parade, as soon as the paraders returned from the cemetery. The whole program was usually about an hour in length, ending at noon – just in time for Chicken-and-Dumplins across the street at the Congregational Church!

wrought iron markers that identified deceased veterans. We were to remove the old flag and replace it with a new one.

For the many war veterans who would march in the parade, it was time to dig out the service uniforms, air them out (for they smelled of moth balls), and – most importantly – make the tiny adjustments so they would fit. For Sanderson Band Director Arch Swift, it meant rehearsing the Sanderson Band in the music they would play during the parade and at any exercises for which the Band had been asked to play.

For the baton Twirlers, uniforms had to be washed and ironed, and twirling skills honed to perfection. For teachers and their students, the approaching Memorial Day meant preparing and rehearsing an exercise in time for the Memorial Day program. For countless others, it meant selecting flowers, bouquets and cemetery tubs to be placed at the family's grave sites.

For the Ladies Circle at the Congregational Church, it meant readying the downstairs room at the church and preparing a meal, most often Chicken-and-Dumplins, timed to be ready to serve by the end of exercises at the Town Hall.

For others, like Malcolm and Pauline Clark, preparations for the day meant polishing and shining the leather saddles and tack for their participation as riders in the parade. For the volunteer firemen, preparations meant polishing the fire engine and cleaning all the gear.

The Baton Twirlers, in the school parking lot, ready for the parade.
Dorothy N. Townsley photo, Author's Collection.

Most years the parade started at the Sanderson parking lot. I usually marched with the Boy Scouts. Shirley was a twirler, so she stepped off with them. At first our formations were a little ragged and the music was a little muddled as we marched out of the parking lot and struggled through a

Column Left onto Buckland Road. Springtime in New England affords little time for such things as learning how to march – and play an instrument at the same time!

By the time we passed the end of Bronson Avenue ("Scrap Alley" to most locals), the Band looked a little better. Maude Roberts was on her front porch, waving. Most any other time she'd be shaking a fist in the air and shouting at the little brats she was convinced were picking on her. She was often right.

The turn onto Main Street went a little better for the Sanderson Band. By now they were seasoned veterans of perhaps two hundred yards. Few marchers or spectators noted the rambling house at the corner of Buckland Road and Main Street, where famed Hollywood director, Cecil B. DeMille, was born in 1881. Most likely, Police Chief Walt Zalenski guarded this or another of the intersections.

Presently the parade passed Ted Day's Store. Pres frequented Ted Day's store. Mother gave him a list, and Pres handed the list to Ted or to his son, Charlie, who scurried around to find what Mother specified. Pres, in the mean time, could visit with whoever was there. Ted and his wife, Mildred, were stalwarts in the community; leaders at the Congregational Church as well as successful business people.

Family folklore maintains that Gramp Nelson wouldn't shop at Day's because, "*He sells liquor!*" You have to whisper that observation, or at least hiss it sotto voce, to invoke the appropriate degree of Nannie and Gramp's righteous Baptist distain. Gramp shopped instead at Elmer's Store a little farther down Main Street.

By now the lead elements of the Band were passing in front of Gil Gardner's Hardware Store, the Post Office and the Library. Gil was another fixture in Ashfield life, a respected businessman and a member of the Rod and Gun Club. Membership in the Rod and Gun Club didn't automatically make you a good person, but it did cut you a little slack if there was some question about your character. Gil, however, like his predecessor, Walter Benjamin, was a genuinely good guy, and his hardware store, at least to this youngster, was a marvel of *stuff*. If it was even remotely hardware, Gil had it. I frequented Gil's most often for ammunition: a box of fifty .22 Long Rifle cartridges cost 50 cents.

Gil Gardner's hardware store occupied the west side of the building; the Post Office occupied the east side. Gil Henry was the postmaster. He and his wife, Lillian, lived down the street a few houses.

The bulk of our short parade had now passed the Belding Memorial Library, directly across the street from the hardware store and Post Office. A large stone edifice facing Main Street, large by Ashfield standards, at least, the library was presided over by librarian Dorothy Craft. Her warm smile welcomed you, and her icy stare hushed your youthful exuberance. The Library was a quiet haven to which our Sanderson teachers shepherded us early each school year.

We were often permitted to walk from the school to the library to work on special projects and reports. The proper route was down the steps to Bronson Avenue, turning left past Ray Reniff's garage and over the little bridge spanning the stream out of Ashfield Lake, then turning right on Main Street in front of Dr. Whittier's. It was a ten minute walk, fifteen if you really milked it, but we often took a shortcut down the bank to the stream, carefully stepping on the stones in the brook, and scrambling up the bank on the other side. There was nothing wrong with this shortcut – except that many of the houses on both sides of the little stream dumped their sewage, raw and untreated, into it! This was still accepted practice in 1950, and you hoped that there had been a rain shower in the not-too-distant past to have washed the banks clean. Still, you had to look closely to make sure the rock you were about to step on wouldn't be squishy and have to be scraped off the bottom of your shoe.

Most of the old-timers who lived at The Ashfield House were lined up on the front porch to watch the parade go by. It was a high point of their year but sadly, few were able to remember it much after the fire trucks, bringing up the rear, had passed from view.

The parade by now was passing in front of Elmer's Store. The store was closed today, first because it was a holiday, and second, because its proprietor was marching in the parade. Elmer Lesure was one of a large contingent of World War II veterans who proudly marched in the Memorial Day parade. Their names represented a cross-section of Ashfield residents: Graveses and Howeses, Halls and Burnetts, and there were a few veterans from World War I as well. While he could, Lucian Robbins, a lanky veteran of the Spanish-American War marched along. We kids stared with curiosity at his uniform, a kind of mustardy brownish with a broad-brimmed Campaign hat.

Elmer's, at the foot of Norton Hill Road where it intersects with Main Street, was then, as now, a crossroads where townspeople met. His was a full service store, featuring meat as well as the usual dry goods. Elmer didn't sell anything alcoholic. He might have, except the entrance to the store was less than 500 feet from the Congregational Church, so the zoning laws prohibited liquor sales. Elmer and his store prospered through the 1950s and into the 1960s before the advent of super markets and better roads to them.

Some years the parade stopped in front of the Ashfield Town Hall for a short speech or recitation, but on this day the parade participants strode right on past it while others inside finished arranging the chairs for the exercises that would follow when everyone returned from the cemetery.

Our parade passed in front of the brand new Firehouse, nestled next to the Town Hall. The Firehouse was built in the late 1950s as quarters for the town's fire truck and new ambulance. As the members of the Sanderson Band marched by, their eyes stole a glance around the Firehouse and its grounds to see if the mischief makers had left any surprises hereabouts. One year, to the organizers' dismay and to the paraders' delight, a horse-drawn sleigh sat atop the peak of the Firehouse roof.

Nearly directly across the street from the Firehouse is the Congregational Church. Nannie and Gramp were regulars here, as were Ruth Clark and Grammie Townsley; Gramp and Nannie most always gave them a ride to church. Mother and Pres went to the Congregational Church, in fact, that's where they were married, not many years earlier, by Reverend Walter Couch.

At the corner of Main Street and South Street sits St. John's Episcopal Church, its structure dating from the 1820s. In 1945 the St. John's vicarate was vacant. At about the same time, Rev. Couch, pastor of the Congregational Church, was called to another church.

Neither church could afford the luxury of separate salaries and the upkeep of separate parsonages, so it was determined to call one pastor/vicar to serve both churches. This practice was not uncommon in either sect, having one person serve "yoked ministries" with two or more churches, but it was unique to link two such divergent groups, Episcopal and Congregational, under a single individual. Rev. Philip H. Steinmetz was called in 1945 to be vicar of St. John's Church and pastor of the Ashfield Congregational Church. Much loved by the parishioners of both churches, Rev. Steinmetz continued to be an influence in Ashfield for many years after he moved on to other callings.

Our parade has passed the now vacant store from which the Rice Brothers, Frank and Pliny, sold meat several years before. New ownership would open the store as a snack bar in the late 1950s. I bought my first pack of cigarettes here, cost me twenty-eight cents. Soon after that, ownership was taken by the Ashfield Historical Society.

Next door, and about opposite St. John's, was Sandberg's Garage, one of three places in town where you could get cars and trucks repaired. The other two? Ray Reniff's on Bronson Avenue and the Ashfield Ford dealership farther west on Main Street.

In the square at the intersection of Main Street, South Street and North Street was a stone structure that was once a watering trough for horses. By the time of our 1950s parade, it was filled in and made into a flower garden.

The parade executed a pretty orderly Column Left onto North Street. The Sanderson Band members and the assorted entourage by now were veterans of nearly a half mile of marching, and were in step, confident and proud.

Band Director, Arch Swift, and Drum Major, Russell Roberts, halted the band at the monument at the corner North Street and Baptist Corner Road. Trumpeter Lenny Graves was quietly dispatched to a position behind the small hill that covers the Cemetery's vault. A couple of the World War II veterans who marched as a color guard quietly stepped aside and waited at attention. We who marched with the Boy Scouts crowded around discreetly.

Despite the presence of many people, many of them youngsters, it was absolutely quiet, save for the breeze rattling the poplar leaves, and the call of a distant crow. The breeze carried the sweet spring country air, a pungence of newly turned earth and lingering blossoms. In the hush, a town official, or perhaps Rev. Steinmetz (he had a "big voice," deep, clear, almost sepulchral – ideal for such an occasion) stepped forth to offer a few words appropriate to the occasion.

The Sanderson Band then offered a nice rendition of the National Anthem, Rev. Steinmetz intoned a benediction, and Lenny Graves, out of sight behind the little hill, played Taps. The contingent from the Color Guard cocked their rifles as one, and began a twenty one gun salute. To this thirteen-year-old, it was the most beautiful thing I'd ever heard, and I was moved to tears then as I have been ever since at such a ceremony.

Memorial Day wasn't the only occasion for a parade. We of Ashfield were happy to find any occasion to parade our civic pride. One such occasion was in 1952, probably the Fourth of July. We in Apple Valley put together a float that involved all the valley's youngsters. Neighbors decorated Pres Townsley's apple wagon, a large flat rig, with a huge apple, probably an assembly of hay wrapped with red paper or cloth. Connie Williams was selected as the Apple Princess, Joy Ann Howes and Pat Graves were her court, and the rest of us were apples in white shirts or blouses wearing red crepe paper caps with leaves to look like apples. Even Pres had an apple cap. Pres drove the wagon with his team, and Harry Williams was the "out-walker," walking ahead of the horses in case a surprise should spook the team. All the Apple Valley youngsters were in that parade. Although they weren't on the float, Fred Scott and Lois Williams were in the band, and Russ Williams played the drum in the band.

Town Hall was a stately typically New England structure. It was constructed in 1812 as the First Congregational Church and was originally located atop Norton Hill at the current Hill Cemetery. About 1865 it was sold to the town and moved down Norton Hill to its present location fronting on Main Street.

Apple Valley Float, 1952. Visible, besides Pres Townsley and his team, are Joy Howes, Bob Bates, Lynn Townsley, Pat Graves, an unknown youngster adjusting cap, Connie Williams, Lois Greenman, Shirley Townsley, Ron Howes and Bill Townsley. Dorothy N. Townsley photo, Author's Collection.

Upstairs in the old Town Hall we quietly took our seats. One Memorial Day, classmate Joe Valliere and I presented a show and tell about the Second World War in the Pacific, complete with maps and other displays.

A notable person in town then offered a short speech. One year the speaker was Superintendent of Schools C. Warren Gardner. Mr. Gardner was well respected in Ashfield where he lived, and in the surrounding communities that made up the local school district. Clear, articulate, well organized, it was the way I wanted to be, later in life, when I needed to present an idea or offer a concept.

Most of the attendees at the Town Hall event now ambled across Main Street to the Congregational Church, downstairs to the dining area in Fellowship Hall. Here the Ladies Circle of the church had prepared a meal, most likely their famous Chicken and Dumplings. Some of our moms and sisters were servers.

We early adolescent boys gazed about, sensing feelings of attraction to the young women, unfamiliar feelings. Nice feelings. These were the same girls we used to pick on and harass, maybe even moments earlier. But now, something we couldn't yet grasp felt *different...*

But now, we devoured the tasty chicken and dumplings and raced off to the next event of the day, the annual Sanderson Academy shootout between the alumni and the current high school baseball team. The game took place at the high school field, a ball field that had an outfield full of challenges.

About fifty feet past first base, right down the right field foul line, was the corner of the Sanderson building. The Principal's office was at the second floor of that corner, and the Principal was known to open his window to watch a game. In the corner a little farther into right field was a large oil tank. Early in the season, and once as late as Memorial Day, there was a big pile of snow that slid off the various roofs in that angle.

Nobody wanted to play right field. Nobody wanted to play first base either.

Centerfield and left field were an adventure, too. There were no fences, so a well-hit ball could fly and roll five hundred feet, into the softball field beyond left field or towards Pat Pollen's house way beyond centerfield.

The game was usually a rout in the mid and late 1950s, with the alumni thoroughly thrashing us undergrads. A team made up of our Scott neighbors, aided and abetted by a phalanx of Graveses and Howeses, clubbed us undergrads mercilessly. A Dubuque laid on a lick or two, even a couple of Rices joined in the fray with line drives into that dreaded right field corner.

Sometimes Memorial Day was warm enough that some of those same adolescents who pondered those strange and unfamiliar feelings at the church dinner not long before began to discuss swimming in the lake. Those discussions usually led one adolescent to dare another to take a dip in Ashfield Lake. That's the same Ashfield Lake that had ice in it only a month before, the same Ashfield Lake into which snow flurries had fallen, sometimes only days before. Nonetheless, bravado trumps reason, and one or more foolhardy young men stripped down and plunged in. An attractive young woman joined the ranks one year, though she rushes to assure us she was properly attired.

All in all, Memorial Day was a grand success. We had paid our somber respects to those who had passed away. We had filled our bellies with great food. We had played a fun, though humbling baseball game. It had been a fun Ashfield day. Now we headed back home to reality, to chores and suppers and bedtime. Tomorrow was another school day, another work day.

Chapter 5
Summer

Many of my contemporaries dreaded the end of school in June. For many of us, some of the girls especially, summer would be a time of little challenge, of laziness - of boredom. For others, mostly the farm kids, it would be a time of very heavy and strenuous work, of long hours and little time for play.

The main feature of summer on the farm in the 1950s was the gathering of feed for the livestock. Filling the silos with grass silage was the first task, and that process began even before school let out. Haying then occupied most of our attention for the rest of the summer. We often had two hay crops – maybe three if you counted silage as one - first cutting and second cutting, usually called "rowen." If there were free days in between hay crops, there were plenty of other tasks, like "nailing boxes" (assembling wooden apple boxes) and hoeing and weeding household gardens.

But one of the great things about summer was that it drew out the "city cousins" to come and help. I'm not sure it was voluntary on the part of the cousins; perhaps it was more a way for their moms and dads to get a little freedom – an answer to their spring-ending, "How am I going to live through a whole summer of having kids around all day?"

Uncle Floyd and Aunt Jane Townsley visited at the Townsley farm often during summers with their kids, Bill, Ginny, Lynn and later, Ricky. Bill moved to Ashfield as a teen and graduated from Sanderson Academy a couple of years after me. He and I grew up more or less together. As pre-adolescents, our comic book hero, Straight Arrow, taught us all about Indian lore. We romped over the fields waving our arms and signaling just as our hero showed us on those Nabisco Shredded Wheat cards.

The Greenman cousins often visited at Nannie and Gramp's farm down the road. They were frequent and welcome companions for playing and fishing.

Well into the 1950s we filled two tall silos with grass to be fed out in the winter as silage to the cattle. The process of filling the silos then was very labor-intensive. Pres mowed the grass using the horse team hitched to a ride-on sickle bar mower. Ralph immediately raked and baled the grass. Those green bales were incredibly heavy, so Ralph would drive up to a bale on his Farmall H with a fork lift on the front and I'd wrestle the bale into the loader. We tried scooping them up with the forks of the loader, but most of the time we'd end up with as much dirt as bale. Ralph dumped the green bales into one of the trucks and drove it to a chopper/blower outside the bottom of the silo.

The chopper/blower was a home-made machine consisting of a conveyor belt onto which you'd drop a bale and quickly cut its twines with a murderous cutter (a knife from the sickle bar of a mowing machine with a six inch or so handle welded to it). The conveyor moved the bale into the chopper, which fed into the blower which blew the chopped grass up an eight or ten inch tube into the silo.

As I look back on it, the whole process was pretty hazardous. The twine cutter was capable of lopping off a finger, for example. As you unloaded the bales onto the conveyor there was always a chance of slipping on the wet grass and being conveyed into the chopper along with the grass. The blower was driven by a foot wide web belt, and though it didn't happen often, the drive belt was capable of slipping off at speed, and was massive enough to have mangled almost anything in its path. Neighbor Clif Scott caught a mittened hand in such a belt once and lost most of his right hand - and nearly his life! That served as visible warning to those of us who used such belt-driven equipment!

As the youngest member of the silage-cutting crew, it was my job to climb into the silo and spread the chopped grass evenly as it was blown in. This avoided air pockets which would not only waste space, but prevent the silage from curing properly. It wasn't too bad a job if you liked to be covered with wet grass in a steamy sauna. The problem was getting in and out of the silo, especially as the level of the grass approached its top. I was uncomfortable with heights and scared to death going up the outside of the silo. The last ten feet or so were above the barn roof. The silo's hoops (the binding rods that encircle the silo to hold it together, like hoops on a barrel) became wider apart at the top.

Coming out of the filled silo was even worse. I had to come out a side of the silo roof and feel my way to the hoops. I'm cringing even as I write this now, over fifty years later! I knew I had to do it myself for two reasons – first, it was a matter of pride. If anyone had to come after me, the ribbing would have been unbearable. Secondly, whoever came after me would have had the same or greater peril. I drew up my courage and slowly climbed down. I don't think I've told this story ever before.

One side effect of filling the silo was the fermentation process. Beginning well before the silo was full, the increasing weight of the silage pressed out all the juices in the grass. The thick liquid oozed from the bottom of the silo. As soon as it hit the air it began to rot – with a stench that was nearly unbearable. With the ooze came flies by the thousands, all attracted to what to them must have been a heavenly aroma. We suffered in silence, aware that this was an unavoidable consequence of the process, and praying for a northerly breeze that would disperse the gawd-awful odor toward Gramp and Nannie's.

To combat the fermentation-drawn flies, Fred installed an electric bug zapper over the screen on the window to the Back Room. It was fascinating to watch flying things meet their Maker on it. Mosquitoes barely made a sound as they hit it. Flies made a quick "fzt," and at night you could see a spark. Moths were a bit flashier, but the big attraction was to toss a grasshopper on the zapper. They sizzled and fried and smoked with an acrid smell I still vividly recall.

Haying was also very labor-intensive. The process began in late June and continued through Labor Day and beyond. The general idea is to mow the hay, dry it, haul it to the barn and mow[13] it away.

Early on there was really only one kind of hay, timothy, with a little orchard grass thrown in. By the mid-1950s we began to plant other grasses, like alfalfa and trefoil. Ralph was particularly taken with trefoil, then newly touted as a high-yield kind of hay. As soon as we finished clearing the field above the blueberry patch, Ralph planted it with trefoil, and long after the trefoil experiment was forgotten, that hayfield was still "The Trefoil Piece."

Most of the hayfields were referred to by their location – "Below the Barn" and "Across the Road," for example. A few of the hayfields, like The Trefoil Piece, had names. "Shangri La" was a ten acre or so lot atop a hill in Buckland. Shangri La was a pleasant place to hay. You could see to the south way up Smith Hill and Hall's farm, almost to Ashfield village. It was quiet there, with only the sound of crickets, grasshoppers, crows and sometimes the squawk of a pheasant. There was always a breeze, a pleasant relief from the merciless sun on a hot July day.

The whole haying process matured as I grew up. I barely remember the early days before baling, of gathering loose hay and drawing it to the barn.

---

13 I've been long puzzled by the word I've spelled as m-o-w. Pronounce it like *blow* and it means to cut the hay (or the lawn, for that matter), but pronounce it like *cow*, it means to store the hay away in that part of the barn called the hay mow.

In the *really* old days, cutting the hay began by gathering as large an army of men as possible, equipping them with scythes and sending them into the field. Mowing with a scythe is an art, from "stoning the blade" to "keeping the heel down," requiring a person with a strong back, strong arms and well calloused hands to be done effectively. Once you got the hang and rhythm of it, you could lay down a sizeable amount of hay in fairly short order. Mercifully, by the time I came along, the only application of that art was applied to mowing under the apple trees in the orchard, or clearing weeds and light brush.

A big load of hay, about 1930. It appears to be Pres on top. Horses and load are between the barn and applehouse, the farmhouse is at the left rear. Neither silo has been built yet.
Unknown photographer, Author's Collection.

In my day, Pres often started the process by mowing the hayfield using the team of horses hitched to that same ride-on sickle bar (or cutter bar) mower. If the hay was standing up straight and there were no obstacles, it was a fairly straight-forward job for an experienced horseman and his team. He might encounter woodchuck holes (a danger to the horses) or woodchuck mounds (which could break the cutter bar). If there's been a recent thunderstorm with heavy wind, the hay may be blown down instead of standing up straight. Blown-down hay frequently twisted and snarled around the cutter bar. When the hay was thick and lush the process became even trickier. It's not an easy task, even using a tractor.

The next step was to dry the newly mown hay thoroughly and quickly. If you didn't, it could spontaneously combust and burn the barn down!

Again, in the *really* old days, drying the hay meant gathering that same army, equipping them with pitchforks and sending them into the field to "turn the hay." The intent here was to move or turn the damper hay into the sun and air where it could dry better. The process was still used from time to time when I began haying, though it had been replaced by a number of mechanical processes that usually succeeded in drying the hay.

So the next step was to "tedder" the hay. We had a horse-drawn machine called a tedder[14]. The tedder was a joy for a youngster to behold. It had a half-dozen hay forks activated by a cam-driven mechanism. When it was pulled across the field, the forks would swirl, kick up and tear apart the mowed hay with gleeful abandon!

As visually pleasing as it was to this youngster, teddering could be destructive, especially to grasses like alfalfa and trefoil, knocking all the good leaves off and leaving just the stalks. Often teddering was not enough to dry the hay. One remedy, or next step, was to rake it.

Early in my haying career, Pres would again hitch the team to a dump rake. The dump rake was a two-wheeled machine, pulled by a team of horses, with a seat from which Pres drove and periodically stepped on a trigger that raised the 20-odd rake tines. He would drive back and forth across the hayfield, raking hay and triggering the dump mechanism to leave the gathered hay in what would become long mostly straight "windrows."

By the early 1950s we had acquired a side-delivery rake, a machine pulled behind a tractor which rolled the hay into windrows. By rolling the hay it was possible to position the least dry hay in the windrow atop the roll in the sun. Not only that but it was gentler on the hay!

It was about then that Ralph made Pres a two-wheeled gig. With the team hitched to the gig, Pres could now pull all the wagons that were designed to be pulled by tractors or trucks. Much as it streamlined many of the tasks on the farm, Pres mourned not being able to use the dump rake any longer, as he and Ralph could never figure out a way to modify the dump rake to hitch it to the gig. Besides, the need for the dump rake was set aside when we got a side delivery rake.

If by now the hay wasn't thoroughly dry, it meant heading to the field with pitchforks to shake out and spread out some of the denser piles. It was here that I learned I was somewhat ambidextrous. With things like handling a pitchfork or shovel or hoe (or hockey stick, for that matter, though I wouldn't learn that for many years) I could hold the shaft with *either* hand closest to the tines. In fact, I had never thought that there was handed-ness to pitch-forking or shoveling or hoeing.

---

14 I'm spelling *tedder* phonetically, as I've never seen the word spelled out

Once the hay was thoroughly dry, Ralph made another quick pass with the side delivery rake, to align the windrows for ease of baling. He then hitched the tractor to the baler.

For the rest of the haying crew, now was the time for a short rest and a drink of water. We would drink a lot – water and "purple poison," a concoction of grape juice, orange juice, ginger ale, etc. One year someone suggested that beer was the best coolant. I was too young to be included in

Pres raking hay on Roundtop. He's pulling a side-delivery rake using the two-wheeled
gig Ralph made up for him.
Dorothy N. Townsley photo, Author's Collection.

the testing process! Beer didn't cool us any more than other drinks - and it kind of decreased productivity!

We loaded the hay bales on either the International truck (with a headboard but no sideboards) or the flatbed trailer that Pres used during apple picking. The trick now was to load as many bales as possible onto whatever conveyance we were using. In a way it was a balancing act – load as many bales as you can without having them fall off the load or tip the vehicle on its side!

Loading was an onerous task. The bales were heavy, up to 60 pounds or more. One side of the bale was the sharp cut ends of the stalks. Loading usually took place at the end of a hot and sticky day. It took a team of workers to pick up the baled hay - a truck driver, a stacker on the bed of the truck, and at least one bale-picker-upper. There was a knack to stacking the bales, interlocking them so they won't come tumbling down.

To qualify as a truck driver, all you needed, after a short lesson, was to be physically able to reach the clutch, brake pedals and the accelerator. It was a good job for a youngster who might not be rugged enough to lift or carry bales of hay. In fact, most farm kids have been driving for several years before they are able to acquire a license. A good driver made the task of loading hay bales onto the truck easier, as the driver could back the rig close to your bale so all you had to do was lift or sling it onto the truck.

The final step in the haying process was to store away the hay in the barn. Hay is stored in most New England barns in the hay loft, the top part of the barn. Most barns took advantage of the hilly terrain with a ramp or some device so you could drive a loaded hay wagon or truck right into the loft. Storing the hay up high made it easier to feed the cattle on the floor below. All one had to do was to drop the hay through a hole in the floor of the loft where it could land close to the cows and be doled out as needed.

In the *really* old days Pres would back the loaded hay wagon up the ramp into the loft. We had a kind of unique device whose name I can't recall for lifting the hay off the wagon and moving it to one end or the other of the loft. Pres would unhitch one horse from the team, "Chub," as I remember, and hitch him to the rope that operated the device. At Pres' signal, Chub would walk down the ramp, then stop at Preston's "Whoa." He'd then turn around and return to his starting point, repeating the process until the wagon was unloaded.

Chub, like all horses, was a creature of habit. He had committed the routine to memory, a fact that enabled even five- and six-year-olds to become part of the unloading process. Pres would seat one of us on Chub's broad back, and we would proudly "drive Chub." Nobody let on to us that Chub was on auto-pilot; no matter what we kids did, he would continue to plod back and forth until an adult hollered, "Whoa!"

With the advent of bales, mowing away the hay in the barn was just the hard work of lugging the bales to the proper place in the loft and stacking them higher and higher toward the rafters. It was, and still is hot, sweaty work in a dusty, confined space. It was here I learned I had, for sure, hay fever. No matter what kind of nose mask and/or anti-histamine I tried, I always came out of the loft sneezing and blowing and weeping. It became bad enough that I was permanently taken off mowing-away duty.

It seemed like every time we had hay down, anywhere between the drying and the into-the-barn stages, a thundershower would come up. You knew, even as a kid, there was a possibility of showers – you could feel it in the air. That, and Bob Steele, the trusted morning announcer at WTIC in Hartford, had forecast it.

Before long you could see real thunder clouds among the scattered "fair weather" cumulus, and soon after, the faint but distinct sound of thunder. Everyone would race for the truck to pick up the hay we'd baled so far. The thunder marched nearer and nearer, and the clouds blackened the northwest sky over Pumpkin Hill. Soon you could actually see the lightning bolts.

As the storm approached, whether we had finished or not, Ralph would race the loaded truck into the slaughter house and out of the rain. Sometimes we covered the loaded truck with a tarpaulin, which proved to be hard job especially in the rising wind. Then as the first drops of rain began to fall (and God help us if those first drops fell as hail) we'd race back to the house.

Once we had dried off a little we'd get a drink (maybe cold grape juice- "panther piss") everyone would head for the screened-in front porch at the end of the house to watch the storm pass. This was one of the special times that we felt at ease with "the grown-ups," probably because together we had come through the gathering storm and together we had done our best to minimize its effects. It's one of my favorite memories of growing up on the farm.

Most thunderstorms passed uneventfully, full of sound and fury, but seldom doing more than messing up a good cutting of hay. Once in a while, though, we'd lose electrical power, sometimes in the middle of milking, thus losing the air compressor and therefore the use of the Surge milking machines. I remember at least once Ralph hooked up a gas-driven compressor in place of the electric one.

Thunderstorms can raise havoc with the apple crop as well. Hail anytime from early June through apple-picking in September and early October can be devastating, denting or puncturing the apples to the point that they may be nearly unsellable. A heavy wind, especially from August on, can knock the apples to the ground or bruise them.

One day Shirley and I were playing in the dirt under the big catalpa tree in front of the house (where the maple tree is now) when a sudden rainstorm or thundershower came up. I remember Mother grabbing a long coat or a blanket over her head and racing from the porch to collect us and shelter us back to the house.

It may seem weird to some, but I always liked thunderstorms. We used to have some good ones in Apple Valley. The biggest and best thunderstorms earned Humdingership. The term was bestowed reverentially, with awe and respect, as in, "Gawd, Bob, *that* was a Humdinger!" That was a real Humdinger the night the bull pen got hit, I tell you!

Good haying weather, by definition, needs ample sunlight and hot weather, and it got pretty hot by mid July. It would get super uncomfortable doing the milking on those hot sticky nights: there was usually no breeze whatever in the barn, making the cows sweaty, too.

The haying crew tried to keep in the shade, but that's a scarce commodity in most hayfields. We boys could remove most of our clothing. We wished the girls could, too, probably about as much as they wished they could. If we had to work - haying, for example, we'd wear jeans (to ward off the sharp cut ends of the hay in the bales) and white shirts (which deterred burning - and which absorbed less heat than darker clothing). One year we tried wearing pith helmets to try to keep cooler. It helped a little. Most of the time I went bareheaded. I had enough hair then not to burn my scalp!

Besides haying, there was a long list of jobs that needed to be done sooner or later.

Most farms at the time had fairly extensive gardens that needed tending. If you didn't have anything else to do (at which suggestion we kids would immediately find something – *anything* – to do!), you were handed a hoe and directed to the garden.

I was responsible for mowing the lawn, which for me it meant pushing the manual, reel mower with its 15" blades across the lawn. We never had a powered mower until well after I left home. I don't remember ever taking the initiative to mow the lawn; Pres or Ralph "suggested" I do it.

By late June, the apple trees that blossomed in May have begun to sprout little green apples. Many twigs have two or more new little apples on them. In mid-June, for reasons I never knew, "nature" thinned out the apples by culling out some among the multiples.

By late June, after the "June Drop," it was time to go into the orchard to remove some of the apples nature had overlooked. The idea behind this is that each apple on the twig must share a more or less finite feed from the twig. By removing one or more of the multiples, you enable the survivors to get larger portions and thus grow bigger. Pres did this with confidence. I hated to thin apples because I was never sure which in the bunch was the puniest and was always afraid I'd remove too many.

In the 1950s an apple farm needed a large supply of bushel apple boxes. Part of the need could be met through recycling last year's supply, but there always was a lot of attrition, mostly through boxes sold with apples in 'em! Making or *nailing* boxes was one of the very few ways a youngster could earn some spending money during the summer.

Pres used to buy apple box makings - two ends, two sides and a bottom - and our job as kids was to nail them together. He (and therefore, *we*) called the collected makings "shooks," or something sounding like that. We had nailing jigs, one double-sided (for two people working opposite one another) and another single one. The jigs held the parts in place while you nailed them.

I earned 3 cents a box. Early the first summer I earned enough to buy my very own radio. I rigged up a long extension cord from the barn to the icehouse where I worked so I could listen to my radio. I did most of the nailing; Bill Townsley did some, and Scott Collins, brother of my first heart-throb, did a lot.

Once when nailing apple boxes (I was 12 or 14), we got to fooling around, seems as though there was Scott Collins, Bill Townsley and me. One of the boys had a BB gun. He climbed up on some of the finished boxes and shot me, commando style, in the chest. The BB went through the shirt, and left an awful welt right in the middle of my chest.

By July and extending well into fall, Mother seemed to be continually canning, first vegetables from the garden, then later, fruits from the orchard. My involvement with canning was most often in gathering the produce. We always had a sizeable garden. It was the source of most of the canned vegetables. First came the peas, which needed picking and shelling, then later the string beans and later yet, the shell beans. Carrots and beets came next. Picking and husking corn was troublesome for me, as I was very allergic to corn pollen. Most often we husked the corn in the barn, feeding the husks to the eagerly awaiting horses and cows. By the Fall we had tomatoes, tons of them, it seemed. The neighbors hated to see us coming to visit bearing more darned tomatoes!

We had a good-sized blueberry patch high up on the side of the hill behind the barn, not far from the sugar orchard. It was never clear why Fred planted the blueberry bushes so far up the hill, but it was always supposed that putting them there would avoid some of the late frosts in the spring.

Pres pruned the blueberries in the late fall or winter and cleaned out the briars and weeds that inevitably creep in over time. By mid-July the earliest of the blueberries ripened, and the various strains kept ripening through mid-August.

Picking blueberries is solitary work, a lonely task I hated when I first started picking as a kid. Pres was the primary blueberry picker, and he thoroughly enjoyed the job. It took me a few years, but I eventually learned what he had known all along: it really is a relaxing job.

For one, the blueberry patch is in one of the most scenic parts of the farm – you can look out across Apple Valley – from Clif Scott's, and Francis and Harry Williams's and beyond, across to Malcolm and Richard Clark's, and across Clark's east orchard to Ridge Hill. For another, it's remote and quiet, a great place to sort out your thoughts and frame your future. Maybe these are the reasons Fred planted the blueberries here!

Don, my son, was 14 or 15 when we went blackberrying one August, ending up at the Hall farm. We had split up – he was a bit farther down the hill and I was at the edge of the hayfield below the barn. I'd gotten into some pretty good picking and had worked my way well into the patch of blackberries. Looking down, I saw with horror I was standing perhaps six inches away from a "white-tail hornet[15]" nest, and sure enough, there were *lots* of hornets flying in and out of the nest. How I got that close without triggering them I'll never know.

I fought the urge to run, and just stood there, pondering what my options were. Surely I could hightail it, but just as surely, the hornets would sting me mercilessly every step of the way. And I'm sure I would begin to swell up and probably begin to have difficulty breathing. There was a real possibility I might die – Gramp Nelson was deathly allergic to bee stings and I could be, too. Was Don capable of driving me to the hospital in Greenfield? Maybe, because he had been driving trucks and tractors on the farm all summer.

But as I stood there for many minutes, the whitetails didn't seem especially excited at my presence. In fact some were lighting on my jeans, using my right knee as a staging area on their way back into the world. After several more minutes I tested moving my right leg back, ever so slowly, and that didn't seem to bother them much. I slowly backed away, one stealthy step at a time, each step wondering what would happen if I lost my footing as I back stepped away from the nest. I got away from them without getting as much as a single sting! I had nightmares about it for a long time after that!

The many tasks of summer could be numbing, both physically and mentally, for a youngster. We welcomed whatever escapes came up.

When it rained you could rest. You couldn't hay in the rain for sure, and the gardens were usually too wet or muddy to hoe or weed. Sure, there were

---

15 A good entomologist will tell you there no such thing as a white tailed hornet. "Bald faced hornet" is the correct name, and they're so called because they have white heads – and abdomens, too. However, "The White-Tailed Hornet" was good enough for poet Robert Frost; it's the way I learned it, and I'm too cantankerous to change now.

tasks that could be done, nailing boxes, for example, but most often it was time to read or play. It was a great time to go fishing if the rain wasn't too heavy.

Often, when haying Shangri-La, Ralph's field atop a hill in Buckland, Aunt Martha and Mother would bring over a picnic lunch. We'd take time out to eat, usually going up to the highest corner under the trees where it was cool. Afterwards we could stretch out in the grass and listen to the singing of cicadas on really hot days.

It was here that I first was introduced to Congo Squares. There was always "Purple Poison," which Wayne Jones, a Clark cousin, called "weasel pee-us," hilarious sounding in his North Carolina drawl.

A favorite place in Apple Valley for picnics or neighborhood get-togethers was "the Picnic Place" on the high point of what is now Rick Smith's orchard. There was a grove of pines, sheltering some picnic tables and a fireplace. Shirley remembers there were Ladies Slippers, and now that she mentions it, I recall them, too, quite a few of them, growing on the slope facing the Townsley's farmhouse. "They" (Harold and Floyd Townsley, Mother remembered) put the old desks they took out of the Apple Valley schoolhouse up in the Picnic Place. There was the back of an old car here, too. You couldn't sit on its seat, though, because it was loaded with hornets.

Pres was very apt to take us on a long drive on Sundays, often with a picnic lunch. I remember going to Whitingham Dam and Lake Sadawga, with its floating islands. I was especially fascinated with the idea that land could float! Still another time we went to Brigham Young's birthplace in Vermont.

Though we weren't regular church-goers, Sunday was usually a time to refrain from doing work. There were lots of exceptions, however: during the haying and apple-picking seasons, we had to take advantage of good weather, no matter what day of the week it was. Besides, farm women usually snorted at the thought of no-work-on-Sunday; their families were just as hungry on Sundays as any other day!

A neighbors' outing, about 1943. Left to right, Olin Graves, Pres Townsley (farthest back),
Lillian Williams, Ted Howes (under the birch), Evelyn Howes, and Margaret Graves.
Unknown photographer, Author's Collection.

Frequently Sunday was a time to visit with the neighbors. Sometimes
they'd visit us, and sometimes we'd visit them. Once in a while our parents
would send us off to the grandparents, then go for a picnic – either by
themselves or with their peers.

After working all day in the hayfield, we'd sometimes go jump in the
brook, or for a real treat, somebody would drive us up to Ashfield Lake.
To *really* go swimming, you had to go to Ashfield Lake. I learned to swim
at Ashfield Lake, at the town beach, through the Red Cross swimming
instruction program.

The brook was too small and too cold, and the ice pond was too muddy.
We did go "swimming" in the brook, but it was usually to jump in and climb
out quickly. Then we'd go to work on some sort of a dam, all the while
swatting those tiny but nasty mosquitoes.

To cool off after a hot afternoon hoeing beans or corn, or after haying,
I'd sometimes skinny-dip in the brook. There were a couple of places in the
brook secluded enough and deep enough to get decently wet. In Ashfield I
always skinny-dipped alone.

As an early teen, one escape was to head for the brook with my fishing
pole and a worm or two. As an older teen, I'd head off with my .22 rifle soon

after supper, hunting for woodchucks. I'll have more on both fishing and hunting later.

By the 1950s, family members had begun to disperse in greater numbers than ever before. Getting together with distant family was always a big favorite of the older adults. We kids looked on these gatherings with a little more reserve – to us these get-togethers were meetings of strangers.

We never took a real "Family Vacation," as either we were in school or Pres was working. Mother, Shirley and I got away several times, though.

For a few summers, right after school let out, Mother, Shirley and I went to Plum Island to visit Aunt Vie and Uncle Harry for a week or so. It was an event we saved up for all year. We'd take an 8:30 am or so train from Shelburne Falls, which got us to North Station about 11. Often we'd meet family friend, Jean Currie, and her three daughters, Joan, Gail and Donna.

On at least one of our trips from Ashfield to Plum Island, we went (with the Currie girls I think) to the Public Gardens and rode on the swan boats. I remember the dirty water and the sweaty operator who pedaled the boat.

One time we went to the newly opened Museum of Science. I was dazzled by the Museum, especially by the model steam locomotives whose wheels and stuff turned when you pushed the button. I purchased a plastic model kit of the newly-launched nuclear submarine Nautilus. Later in the afternoon, we boarded another train for the ride to Newburyport. I can still see Aunt Vie and Uncle Harry standing at the station waiting for us. I remember, too, the ride across the causeway to Plum Island, where if you knew just where to look, you could see their cottage from way back near the airport.

By August, the summer evenings became noticeably shorter and somewhat cooler. It took a little longer to dry the hay. Blueberry season petered out. Pres started putting out apple boxes in the orchard for the upcoming picking season.

Summers for us farm kids flew to an abrupt ending with Labor Day. For all of us, farm kids and townies as well, Labor Day came as a relief, relief from boredom for a few, relief from grueling hard work for us farm youngsters. Despite what the calendar said, summer ended with the arrival of the school bus on the Wednesday morning after Labor Day.

Chapter 6
Autumn

There was no gradual slide into autumn. Labor Day was a switch, and with the throwing of that switch the routine of summer suddenly became the drama of school and the fall season.

Three things happened in the fall. A new school year began. The harvest was gathered and stored away. Preparations for winter were completed. Occasionally, something remarkable happened.

Many of us Ashfield kids looked forward to the start of school again. Not me. But like it or not, the Wednesday after Labor Day marked the beginning of the new school year. For me it ended the fraternity of haying. It began a time when I had to prove myself again, before a new teacher, with a new set of expectations. But almost as soon as school began, it was time for Greenfield Fair.

The first event of autumn was Greenfield Fair, the closest we ever got to a carnival or amusement park. Though its formal name was, and still is, *"The Franklin County Fair,"* all of us from nearby towns knew it, and eagerly awaited it, as plain old "Greenfield Fair." It sometimes called just "The Fair," but never "*The* Greenfield Fair."

Though many others did, we never exhibited animals at the Fair.

For a few years in the early 1950s, Mother sold African Violets at Greenfield Fair, at a booth in the Fish and Game building. It was especially fun to visit her there, because not too far from her booth were the series of aquariums with samples of local game fish. I found the big brook and rainbow trout and others to be fascinating. One year the Fish and Game folks had a real live fawn in one end of the building. Shirley was enthralled with the little deer.

Pres and many of the other adults looked forward to the horse and ox draws – and to the free-flowing camaraderie and liquid refreshment that accompanied them. Grandparents and others prepared for the agricultural exhibits, gathering the largest pumpkins and the choicest canned vegetables for display and contest. We kids could barely wait for the midway.

The rides on the midway at Greenfield Fair were tame by today's standards, now that I think about them, everything from a carousel to a Ferris wheel. I don't remember a Tilt-A-Whirl; perhaps they hadn't developed one portable enough to move along the fair circuit. There were lots of "skill" games - coin tosses, ring tosses, baseball throwing - all those games that looked so easy but really were stacked against you. Most everything cost a dime or a quarter.

One of the big thrills for a young teenager at Greenfield Fair was the Joie Chitwood Auto Thrill Show. It was one event we'd save up for throughout each summer. Francis and Lillian Williams took Russell and me to Greenfield Fair one September evening in 1952. Even though Russ and I did everything together that evening, he came down with polio but I didn't. For years, we thought it was that evening that he got polio. But Russell now believes that it was a few days earlier, at another picnic, that he contracted polio.

One fall in the early 1960s, Pres asked me to take his truck and haul an ox team to Greenfield Fair. The teamster was an older man from Buckland, perhaps named Purinton. I was scared to death that I might do something wrong and screw up his prized team, or damage Pres' truck. The old man must have trusted me though: he asked me to be the one to hitch the team to the stone boat.

Cummington Fair has always been one of my favorites. It precedes Greenfield Fair by about three weeks, so, by my definition above, is technically still in the summer. Cummington's is an old-fashioned country fair, with a small midway, lots of agricultural displays and exhibits, and many vendors of country doodads. It had a pretty good ox draw and horse draw, and it was one of Pres' favorites, his last hurrah before apple-picking began.

And did Pres ever hurrah at Cummington Fair! When I was old enough, he would drive to the fairgrounds, then hand me the car keys as we stepped out of the car. Pres knew most of the horsemen at the fair, and most of them invited him in for a quick whiskey. Later in the evening, after the draw was over, I'd go find Pres, coax him back to the car, and listen to him laugh and sing all the way back to Apple Valley. I understood without saying that what happened in Cummington stayed in Cummington.

Because we grew apples, I never had much choice about picking apples! I don't recall that it was too oppressive. In fact, I sort of liked it, because I was treated as an equal, as an adult.

In the 1950s there were several working orchards in Apple Valley. Townsley's was one; it included the small orchard that went with Gramp Nelson's farm. Richard Clark had a large orchard. It included the apple trees around the Clark farmhouse as well as the East Orchard that he had been working to expand for a number of years. Williams's had a small orchard for a while. Ted Howes had a moderately sized orchard, which he greatly expanded when Donald Howes retired in the early 1950s. Neighbor Ed Scott had sizeable orchards in nearby Buckland. Pres gave up tending his orchards in the early 1980s. It about broke his heart.

In 1962 Richard built an apple storage building just above my folks' house. Finished in time for the 1962 season, it was three quarters straight cold storage and the other one quarter was state-of-the-art controlled atmosphere storage. In the "CA room," as it was called, the air in the room was regulated to reduce the oxygen content. It was big enough that he rented out space to Pres and to Ed Scott for their apples.

Raising apples was a year-round job for Pres, but until Fall, it was pretty much a one-man job. In late August I helped Pres get the picking sacks and the wooden ladders out of storage overhead in the sugarhouse. It was hotter than sin under that sugarhouse roof, and there were apt to be hornets nested in the rafters. Fortunately the ladders came out easily, and we inspected them as we pulled them out.

We used all wooden ladders, mostly 20 footers, with a couple of 18s. There was one hefty 24 footer with a kind of a wave at its top, affectionately known as "The Snake." There was also a 22 footer that was twisted at the top; it was "The Corkscrew." The ladders were about 18" wide at the bottom, tapering to a point at the top. Each year there was some attrition – broken rungs and once in a while a broken ladder.

All our ladders were made of poplar, a light and flexible wood that grows all over New England, and spruce rungs. Hal Dodge from Buckland made our ladders. He started by cutting down a poplar tree of about the right height. After it was thoroughly dry, he drilled holes for the rungs, and then sawed it in half lengthwise. Next came the insertion of the rungs and attachment of a pair of spikes at the bottom.

Beginning about the first of September Pres began distributing those bushel apple boxes throughout the orchard. I always marveled at how he always guessed correctly, within a box or two, how many boxes to leave at each tree. He would peer at the tree and its load of apples and announce, "Leave eight bundles [three boxes to a bundle] here. Looks like ten there." And we seldom had too few or too many.

Pres had been lining up apple pickers all summer. Early on our pickers were neighboring farmers who looked forward to extra cash. By the late 1950s the number of working farms had decreased and with them, the number of available farmers decreased, too. We then had some retired men as pickers. And there were always high school boys who would pick from after school until dark.

Drawing apples to Clark's storage, about 1960.
Dorothy N. Townsley Photo, Author's Collection.

Occasionally some out-of-work laborers asked if we needed help, with the only conditions being that they would be paid cash, under the table – and they needed Thursday mornings off to go to the Unemployment Office! We hated to take them, but in the early 1960s we became desperate enough to accept these requests.

We were pressured by the Commonwealth of Massachusetts in the early 1960s to hire unemployed guys from the unemployment office. We tried a couple of times, but the guys never lasted more than a day, sometimes less. We figured they found it too hard to pick apples.

I didn't always like picking apples. I still remember the very first time. Pres set the ladder and I gingerly climbed up a couple of rungs and about froze, barely able to reach out to the nearest apples. Did I ever get razzed by the other apple pickers! Bump Valiton was merciless, and cousin Francis Willis wasn't much better.

In the fall of 1962, when I had returned from working at the Ferguson ranch in Wyoming, Pres put me right to work in the orchard. I soon sort of eased into being the orchard boss. Pres was content to let me direct the crew while he, with the team, hauled the full bushel boxes of apples to the Clark's storage. It was a heady experience for me, then not quite 22, to be so trusted, especially where Pres and I hadn't seen eye-to-eye too well until then. For me it was a special moment.

Our crew that year included Nelson Graves, a pipe-smoking retired farmer and a close friend of Gramp Nelson; Lester "Red" Clark, who worked more or less full time for Pres, Jordan Monohon off and on; and another guy who had been laid off from the electric company. In addition, there were lots of guys from high school in the afternoons. On weekends there were many one-time farmers who now worked at Kendall Mills, Lamson-Goodnow, Greenfield Tap and Die and other nearby businesses.

Pres paid his help by the hour, unlike many other apple growers, who paid by the bushel. Pres told me he paid that way because by-the-bushel pickers bruise more apples in their haste for quantity.

The electric company guy didn't work out well. He was slow and, like many new pickers, set the ladders way too shallow. There's a happy medium that you find as you gain experience between too steep (where you and your ladder could tumble over backwards!) and too shallow, which puts great stress in the legs of the ladder. I warned this guy several times, as had others of the crew, but he persisted. Sure enough, one afternoon before long we heard a crack and sure enough, down he went, gripping for dear life the now top half of the broken ladder. He wasn't injured, but I kept him picking from the ground for the rest of the afternoon. He never showed up again after that.

I saw Pres come off a ladder only once. He had set his ladder in the inside of the tree so he could reach a few apples at the very top of the tree – and the very top of his ladder. As he picked the apples, it lightened the load on the branch until suddenly the branch sprung upward and the ladder started down! I glanced over, and there Pres was, arms and legs all thrashing in the air, and I thought for a moment he was treading air! He was able to catch on to a more substantial limb on the way down, and he hung there while we set a ladder back under him so he could get down. And remarkably, he hadn't bruised a single apple!

From time to time, Red Clark would be joined by his wife, Jean. The two of them were efficient, effective pickers, but they would often bicker with each other and yarn and joke with others of the crew. Red was a long, lean, red-haired lumberman, and Jean was a French-Canadian-speaking Indian from Quebec. Mother had helped her at one time to learn English, but her language was still filled with lots of strange words. Later I learned that most of them were swear words, and she could, when she was perturbed, string together quite a stream of them! She had a fiery temper and a quick sense of humor, making it was great fun to work with her.

I enjoyed the few times I worked with Nelson Graves. He had known my dad well, and he would tell me stories about him. How I wish now I had paid more attention – written down some of what he told me! But I was immortal then, and I guess I thought everybody else was, too.

For several years Pres hired Howard Hall, one of my Rice cousins and an old family friend. Howard was a retired farmer and woodsman, and he worked well with the horses. In fact, he was one of a very few Pres trusted with the team. Howard was quiet, like Pres, and easy-going and patient, unlike Pres. My kids thought he was great, as Howard indulged them with rides on the wagon and letting them help him "drive" the team.

Pres and I seldom picked together, as he most often was busy hauling apples to the storage. In the summer of 1983, Pres had rented the orchards to Ed Pape, and Pape hired Pres as a "consultant," most often as a picker. I helped on weekends.

While working for Pape, Pres and I started picking on the same tree one afternoon. The tree was a moderate-sized Macintosh and it was loaded. Pres and I set our ladders next to each other at about the same time, and he worked clockwise around the tree, while I went counter-clockwise. About half-way around I noticed he was about opposite me, and for some reason I noticed we had picked exactly the same number of bushels. I furtively glanced at him, just in time to catch him just as furtively checking my progress. About then it occurred to me that I probably ought not to let that 74-year-old best this 42-year-old, else I'd never hear the end of it. I picked up my pace a little, and when I glanced over again, I noticed he had too! Soon I noticed just the hint of a wry smile on his face, and I couldn't help but grin, too. We ended up side by side again, fairly scrambling up and down our ladders. We finished the tree tuckered out but with exactly the same number of filled boxes. He wordlessly grinned and nodded, I returned the acknowledgement, and we went on to other trees. Neither of us spoke of it for several years, but he quietly chuckled when I repeated the story for his fellow Oakside retirees at Zephyrhills, Florida.

Early every November, Gramp Nelson banked the lower walls of his house, where the fieldstone foundation was exposed, with leaves. He put them there as insulation, I suppose, to keep the wind from blowing through the cracks and spaces between the fieldstones.

Gramp would cut a strip of tarpaper about a foot wide and stake it on edge about a foot out from the wall. He'd fill this trough with leaves - there were plenty! - then hold the leaves in place with a wooden slat cover on which rocks or bricks were placed to hold them down. I helped him once in a while. And every May, Gramp would reverse the process.

Up the road at the Townsley farm, October was time to get out the storm windows, wash them, and hang them in place over the permanent double-hung windows. Hanging them was no small task. Each storm window weighed in the neighborhood of fifteen pounds, and to install them, you raised the bottom sash of the double hung window, grasped the storm window firmly in both hands, carefully fed it through the opened sash, then leaned out far enough to see to hook the eyes at the window tops over the hooks on the side of the house. By the time you finished hanging all 33 of them (17 upstairs and 16 down, as I recall), your wrists, forearms and back were pretty tired out.

All autumn produce for the winter was added to the fruit cellar under the milkroom at the end of the house. The fruit cellar was a dank, dark and forbidding place lit by a single electric bulb you had to fish for in the dark and twist in its socket to turn it on. A single small casement window, covered by a rusty screen, provided ventilation in the summer, but we sealed it with a bale of hay to insulate it during the winter. A floor, constructed of widely spaced planks on cinder block risers, rested on the dirt subfloor. There was usually an inch or two of water under the planks, part of the natural drainage which flowed off the hill behind the house, through the cellar and out a drain at the far end of the cellar. If you weren't careful, fishing for that light bulb in the dark, you could easily step between the planks into ankle-deep – and very frigid – water!

We stored a couple of apple boxes full of yellow winter squash, blue hubbard squash and a few pumpkins (Grammie Townsley made the absolute best squash and pumpkin pies!), but mainly there were apples. The main content of the fruit cellar was many bushels of apples. Some we sold to customers who stopped by, but many were kept for family usage. We kept a few turnips (though God only knows why!) and several heads of cabbage elsewhere in the cellar, near where the canned fruits and vegetables were kept. There was also a large covered crock in the fruit cellar, full of evil-looking brine in which languished the salt pork for baked beans, a regular staple at our house. When Mother started to get ready to bake beans, I usually headed off to do chores or something, *anything* to get out of having to go to the crock, fish out the slimy salt pork from the brine and slice off a piece for the beanpot.

The day of the Worcester tornado in 1953 was pretty wild in Ashfield, too. As I remember, Bill Craft was visiting, and we were getting the cows in from the pasture above the sugarhouse. The wind howled and the lightning and thunder crackled, but I don't think it rained much. Shirley remembers being at Sue Craft's. She and Sue were walking toward the cemetery when it started raining huge raindrops. Thelma Tobias, Ashfield's telephone switchboard operator at the time, called everyone in town to warn them that a tornado had been forecast.

I was 13 when Hurricane Carol hit in late August 1954. I listened to Don Kent on WBZ radio as he tracked it. It was pretty windy and wet. It blew down one of the pear trees above the apple house and many limbs in the apple orchard. It killed the apple crop that year. Shirley was visiting Sue again, and remembers Pres picking her up in the car and threading his way through the downed branches as they drove home. It blew down the new TV antenna that Floyd had set up near the pear trees a year earlier and Ralph had tried to maintain.

In the fall Boy Scouts started up again. I was a Boy Scout for a while. We'd sometimes go camping. Once we went up to Mt. Ascutney in Vermont. I forgot to bring any silver so I whittled a spoon with my jackknife and got along fine. I think it was on this trip that some of the group decided that instead of hiking along the road down from the top, they'd sneak through the woods along the side. As they did, the first guy in the line brushed up against a hornet nest; he got by just fine, but each kid that followed him got walloped. I remember seeing those boys come flying out of the trees whooping and hollering, trying to escape the hornets.

Another time we camped out at the Ashfield Rod and Gun Club in the late fall or early spring. Bill Craft was my tent-mate. We woke up to snow on the tent.

On one of the campouts I learned to make Welsh Stew. It was the essence of simplicity: Fry some hamburg, add a can of tomato soup and a can of beans. You could add a chopped or cut-up onion for flavor if you felt like it.

Autumn brought with it several holidays. October 12, Columbus Day, was observed, usually with an article or two in the school's Weekly Readers. We read with wonder about the reportedly huge parades in Boston and New York. We might have done something more in Ashfield but few people ever seemed very excited about the date or event.

For us, at least, Halloween was a very minor holiday. We carved jack-o-lanterns and put candles in them, but I don't remember any trick or treating or such as a youngster. Things got wilder as we got older, but all the good things happened while I was away at college.

Every November 11 we observed Armistice Day, the anniversary of the end of World War I. It usually involved exercises at school.

For many years it was Thanksgiving at Nannie and Gramp's. Gramp hauled in card tables and whatever else he could find that was flat enough and broad enough, and set up a long, makeshift table that one year ran from the dining room and through the length of the living room.

Nannie found table cloths, bed sheets were pressed into use one year, and between Nannie's tableware and what she borrowed from us, the Thanksgiving table was set for the multitude. And a multitude it was! It included Gramp and Nannie, us "upstairs Townsleys" and Grammie Townsley (who made the best squash and pumpkin pies ever! I said that before, didn't I! Well, she *did*!!). Aunt Floss Greenman and her kids came from their home in Orange – and often there were more. The first year I worked at Metcalf and Eddy in Boston I brought a co-worker who was from Sao Paulo, Brazil. Sometimes one or another of Gramp's or Nannie's family would happen by.

Gramp lead the meal by saying grace, the grace with the words, "for earthly bounty," that grace I can *almost* hear today. One year Gramp asked me to say the blessing before the meal. I was 12 or 13 or so… I carefully made up a prayer, making sure it had lots of *Thees*, *Thous* and *Shalts* so God would know I knew His language. I also wrote it down in my best penmanship, in case God thought neatness counts.

We had "typically New England" fare – turkey and stuffing, mashed potatoes and gravy, sweet potatoes (only at Thanksgiving!), cranberry jelly slices cookie-cuttered in the form of a turkey, squash, turnip (Pres liked it; I never touched the stuff - couldn't get past the smell!), and other garden vegetables. There was apple cider, milk or water. Dessert was also traditional: Grammie's pumpkin and squash pies (she made the best… oh, I told you that already), apple pie, sometimes a mincemeat pie, and the very best of all, gingerbread with egg sauce!

Uncle Ralph Townsley had a Thanksgiving tradition: he went bird and squirrel hunting after the Thanksgiving meal. A couple of years I went with Russell and him. We usually made a pass through "the Liscomb," a quiet meadow between the gravel pit and Halls off Smith Hill Road. Ralph pondered the name, "the Liscomb," and was frustrated that few but he and Pres had any knowledge of where it was, much less where the name came from. The Liscomb was almost a magical place, a football field sized meadow that had once been a pasture, surrounded by magnificent hemlocks and now-bare maples, and oaks whose withered brown leaves rattled in the occasional breeze. There was an awed silence here, and if we spoke, it was softly, quickly, almost apologetically.

A remarkable thing happened one Thanksgiving, one which confirmed my emerging pride in my Ashfield roots, and of its people and their principles. On Thanksgiving Day, 1954, Apple Valley neighbors Charlie and May Nadeau's house burned. It was an event that clearly defined for me all that is good about a small town. Charlie had banked the fire in the wood space heater in the living room prior to leaving with May and daughter Jean, and apparently, in doing so, a spark fell onto the carpet. It lay there smoldering as the three left for Thanksgiving dinner with their son, Alfred, in Greenfield.

We had been to Roberts's for Thanksgiving that year, and I still vividly remember seeing the blaze as we drove out of the woods near Tanner's on the way home, and hearing Pres' and Mother's wails of horror at Charlie and May's misfortune.

Even before the embers of the Nadeau farmhouse were cold, the neighbors began to pitch in. The next day we opened up Gramp and Nannie's house – they had left by then to spend the winter with Aunt Vie and Uncle Harry at Plum Island – and that day Charlie, May and Jean moved in. Charlie and May were about the same size as Gramp and Nannie, so even the clothes could be shared. Over the winter Pres and Harry Williams and others cut logs which they traded with local saw mills for seasoned lumber, and by mid-summer a new house had been raised, mostly by volunteers, on the foundation of the old.

Autumn could be described in smells, too. Obvious was the smell of apples – from the sweet aroma of a bushel box of Macintosh apples to the crisply pungent scent of a box of Northern Spy apples. Less known was the pervasive smell - and stickiness - of newly dropped nuts from the butternut trees by the applehouse, which most often you learned of when you went to wash the stickiness from your hands.

Autumn, which had started so abruptly the day after Labor Day, was stealthily overtaken by Winter. There was no signal date or event which heralded the end of Fall. Fall faded into oblivion sometime after Thanksgiving, after deer hunting, after the cellar was full of chunk wood and an ample store of stove wood was fully replenished. We seldom got to bid farewell to Autumn as it slunk away, hidden in the gloom of shortened days and the swirling snowflakes.

Chapter 7
Winter

Winter sneaked in clinging to the coattails of Autumn, blowing in with the winds of November, and sifting in on the first tentative flakes of snow. Some time in those blurred days from Thanksgiving to Christmas, Winter drifted in and became a reality, marked by numbed fingers but masked by minds preoccupied with thoughts of Christmas and a new year.

Most often Winter creeps in, with flurries as early as Columbus Day, and sometimes measurable snow by Thanksgiving. Despite what the calendar said, it was a stark reality by early December. Most of us hunkered down for the long, bleak and desolate eternity that was winter.

Winters were to be endured. While youngsters found escape in school, adults grimly set about trying to survive until spring. And being New England adults, they worried. They worried alone. They fretted in pairs. They despaired in groups. Was there enough fire wood? Would the frost be deep enough to freeze the water pipes coming down the hillside from the spring? Did we cut enough silage and hay to get through? Did we put up enough vegetables during the summer? What illnesses might we encounter?

There's a magic moment just as it starts to snow, when it's perfectly still, and the utter quiet might be broken perhaps by the chipping of a chickadee. The snow starts to sift down, and there's almost a hiss as the flakes strike the oak leaves which still clutch the branches.

The worst winter storm I can remember as a child was probably about New Years of 1947/48. I was seven at the time, a first grader. They called out a special snowplow called "the butterfly" to open up the roads. It was orange with a centered plow and wings to roll back the banks at the edge of the road. It went real slow.

One winter we had a big snow drift just behind the applehouse, big enough that Shirley and I could tunnel through it. We dug out sizeable rooms (big to us anyway) and I had a window in one little cave, and glazed it with a sheet of ice. The most remarkable thing that I recall was how quiet it was. It smelled so clean, at least when you first dug it out.

We tried making an igloo, but never figured out how to vault the ceiling. We did a good job with the sides, but when it came to curving it in to close the top, we failed miserably. We made some dandy snow forts and stocked them with a big supply of snowballs, but other than throwing snowballs at one another (which was frowned on!), Shirley and I had no one to have a snowball fight with.

Shirley and I each had sleds. Mine was bigger and clunkier than Shirley's little Flexible Flyer. Every time I could I took her sled. The premier sled run began at the brow of Roundtop, and if the surface of the snow pack was right you could slide from there clear through the front yard and into Apple Valley Road. We seldom dared go into the road out of respect for oncoming traffic. Sometimes the snow would be drifted, making for some dandy jumps.

Pres urged us to try riding one of several jumpers we had at the farm, as it had been a lot of fun for him as a youngster. A jumper is essentially a seat mounted on a runner. I never got the hang of keeping it upright long enough to get much of a run on one.

Shirley and I skated at the ice pond way out back of the barn. At one time the farm cut ice from this man-made pond, but by the early 1950s it had pretty well silted up. Still you could skate on it, but it was apt to be pretty bumpy. It was fed by run-off from the pasture on the side hill above it.

I had a pair of old hand-me-down skates that were too big, so I stuffed a pair of socks in the toes and wore several pairs of heavy socks to get them to fit. Shirley had fussed for a new pair, and when Mother and Pres said they couldn't afford them, Grammie Townsley bought them for her.

Pres grew Christmas trees "up at the Brown Place." The Brown Place was an abandoned farm atop the ridge about a mile or so above Williams's and Nadeau's. The farmhouse remained, but the barn and outbuildings were long since tumbled down. Pres had planted a few hundred Douglas fir seedlings each year for several years, and his Novembers and very early Decembers were consumed by Christmas tree harvest. My involvement was minimal, helping cut trees and evergreen brush on weekends – and planting seedlings in May.

Ted Howes and I worked together for Pres one early December weekend, baling hemlock and spruce greenery, while Pres drew out the branches and twigs he and Ted had cut during the week. Ted began to tell about hanging around with my dad when they were teens, how they drove all over, to dances and the like. It was fun for me to hear of my dad, not as a statistic but as a real young man not a whole lot different from me.

There are several standout memories of winter, memories that only farm folks are privileged to have. As a teenager, we had a cold spell of several days when the temperature was 20 below and it was windy. It was especially hard doing chores, as everything liquid began to freeze solid.

You can tell when it's really cold. As you first step out into the cold, that first breath you inhale freezes the hairs in your nose. Next time you'll remember to wrap a scarf over your mouth and nose and ears. Even that won't help those of us who wear glasses – as you exhale your glasses fog up. The extreme cold even affects the sound of the snow. If it's *really* cold the snow squeaks instead of crunching as you walk through it.

Pres' main job during the winter – in fact, from right after the end of the apple season – was logging. Most often he had at least one other man working for him. Red Clark was one, Walt Graves was another, Godfrey Ice worked a couple of winters, and there were others whose names escape me now. It was tough, dangerous grueling work for little pay and most guys only lasted a season, if that. With schoolwork, I never worked with Pres in the wood lots.

Pres owned a handful of woodlots. Many of them were steep and hilly, terrain that the mechanized loggers would have trouble working. Pres, with his team of horses, could work with relative ease. He typically would work a several acre woodlot over a season, cutting the mature trees and avoiding the younger trees that he might be harvest ten years or more later on. He had two or more power saws which he himself despised, though he recognized they were a lot more efficient than the one- or two-man crosscut saws he used as a youngster.

The harvesting process began with cutting down a tree. Pres, who was uncannily proficient in aiming the tree to be cut, would notch out the tree in the direction he wished it to fall, using a double-bitted axe (or later, the chain saw). Then he went around to the other side of the tree and started sawing through the trunk toward the notch. Finally there was a suspenseful moment in which the tree began, almost imperceptibly at first, to lean and then to fall. And, no, we didn't holler, "Timberrrr!"

At that first hint of "the lean," it's wise to shut off the power saw and step back several feet and be ready to spring out of the way. In the absence of the roar of the chain saw, there is absolute awesome silence in the forest at this moment, save for a gentle breeze or the twitter of a far-off chickadee. It is a reverent moment, poignant because it marks the death of this sturdy giant that has grown here and survived wind and snow and parasites for many years.

Several things can occur beginning in this moment, and only one of them is good. The desired end begins with a crackling overhead as some limbs break as they brush past neighboring trees, and sometimes a creaking and popping as those last few uncut splinters at the stump bend and break, and finally the crashing thump as the tree strikes the ground. However, if the notch was incorrect, or if there was an unexpected breeze – or if the Gods of the Forest decreed - the tree would not fall where it was supposed to.

One big log! Pres was proud of this one. Team doesn't appear to be impressed. That's the icehouse behind the load, farther back is the woodshed.
Unknown photographer, Author's Collection.

The tree top *could* get lodged in its neighbor's branches, never hitting the ground. This is bad because the task of freeing the tree from where it is lodged can be extremely dangerous – you never know which is the last cut that will free the lodged top, and you could easily get crushed (with a roaring power saw at your side!) under the tree trunk or tree top.

The tree *could* fall on your lunch bucket, or on your other tools, or, God forbid, on the horses or on the hired man! Another possibility, if the tree begins to fall before enough of the trunk is cut through, the butt of the tree can splinter with a crack, spraying splinters in any direction!

The next step is to cut the tree trunk into saleable logs, the longer, the better, into lengths of between 8 and 16 feet. First in the process is to "limb out" the fallen tree – that is, to cut off all the branches up to the point at which no more saleable logs may be cut. This is done with the chain saw or with an axe, and the axes we used were light double-bitted axes – that is, they have two murderously sharp blades.

At this point, Pres would "snake out" the logs from where they lay to the nearby logging sled. He unhitched one of the horses from the sled and attached one of the eveners to the tugs, and drove or led the horse to the appropriate log. He would then hook one end of the logging chain around the log, the other end to the evener, and with a chirp to the horse and a flap of the reins, the horse would "snake" the log to the side of the logging sled.

Any youngster growing up on a farm is expected to help out with the day to day chores. Feeding the calves is the earliest task I remember. It's often the first task a youngster is assigned. It takes a moderately strong back to lug the pails of milk, milk supplement and water.

More importantly, it also takes a strong will, because the calves soon weigh as much and more than the youngsters feeding them. A thirsty calf most likely has lazed around all day conjuring up ways and methods of getting at the contents of the bucket. By feeding time she is a plunging, lunging bundle of muscle and sinew, eager to suck anything in sight – the nipple on the pail, the fingers of the youngster who is trying to entice the calf to drink from the pail, the youngster's jacket or hat or mittens. To Mother's dismay, Shirley and I lost several mittens in the barn over the years.

Watering the team of horses – and Lady, Shirley's mare - was a next assignment. The task also took the same strong back and arms, and it took a youngster that was a little taller to swing the heavy water buckets over the edge of the horse manger. It took the same determination as when feeding the calves, as a horse isn't a whole lot brighter than those silly calves. In his eagerness to get his nose into the full pail of water, a horse was likely to knock it aside, often spilling it all over the unfortunate water carrier.

Pres usually fed the horses, first their oats and grain ration, then, just as chores were about ended, a slab or two of baled hay. I was finally judged fit enough to feed the horses after I had spent my first summer tending horses with Pete Bundy at Naushon Island.

Mucking out the horses was one of the tasks I was assigned. It involved taking a broad shovel behind the horses and filling a large tin basket with horse buns (manure) and wet sawdust bedding, then dumping the bucket load down one of the scuttles into the manure pit. The final step in mucking out the horses is to get a basket or two of sawdust to spread under the horses.

Working behind horses that were tied up in their stalls was not without hazard. Pres had a couple of horses that were apt to kick, and with the heavy calked horseshoes, it could be a deadly job. I learned early on that it was wise to let the horses know you were stepping in behind them. Surprise a horse and all hell could break loose! At least one of his horses took exception to having someone step into the stall beside him, lashing out by "cow-kicking" (kicking forward with their hind feet) or leaning against the intruder, squashing him against the wall of the stall.

Mucking out the cows and calves was another of the jobs assigned to a youngster once he or she was physically big enough to effectively use a hoe and a shovel. The principle of this task is to move all the cow manure and wet sawdust bedding to the scuttles and into the manure pit below.

It's a job that has a lot of seasonal variability to it. In the winter the cow flaps tend to be more or less solid, thus making them easier to shovel. However, the cows were kept stanchioned (tied up) in the barn during the winter, so there was a lot more manure to be cleaned up. Not only that, but some of the cows objected to being disturbed by an upstart youngster bearing a hoe, and sometimes lashed out with a flying hoof or, more often, a swinging, manure encrusted tail.

In the summer a new set of dynamics sets in. We began to turn the cows out into the barnyard and pasture in late May. That afforded them exercise and some nice new green grass. On the up side, for a neophyte mucker, at least, there is less manure to clean out. On the down side, that nice new green grass is a powerful laxative, so the manure to be moved is very liquid!

A follow-up chore to mucking out both the cattle and the horses was to spread clean sawdust bedding where needed. The sawdust serves a couple of things – first, it's cleaner than the urine-soaked stuff you just mucked out, and second, it tends to soak up any urine that missed the gutter.

Townsleys got their sawdust from any of several local sawmills. There were many of them around with owners who were only too happy to have you take a truckload away. Getting sawdust was a hard job. It was all hand work loading the sawdust into the truck using as big a scoop shovel as you could handle, then repeating the process unloading it back at the barn.

We stored our sawdust in a large bin in a corner of the hay loft. You could drive the truckload of new sawdust fairly close to it, making unloading the sawdust a little easier. We had a nearby scuttle in the floor of the hayloft through which we could drop enough sawdust into a bin on the main floor where it would parceled out as needed.

Getting sawdust down from the hayloft was a pleasant task, especially in the winter. Because the sawdust was usually a little damp when we picked it up at the sawmill, it was often warm due to slow oxidation, and the steamy warmth was welcome on a frigid winter evening. Not only that, but it smelled nice, too. The sweet smell of newly cut wood and sawdust is hard to describe – and equally hard to forget!

Often, while we youngsters were up in the hayloft getting down sawdust, we were asked to get down a bale or two of hay. It couldn't be just *any* hay – it had to be "from that batch of rowen we cut just before Labor Day." I always had an awful time trying to figure out which bales were asked for. It all looked the same to me. Oh, I could tell rowen from first cutting, but, beyond that, I was in trouble. As I look back on it, there was little way I could have known which was which, as I could never be part of the mowing-away process because of my hay fever.

Youngsters were seldom asked to distribute the hay to the cattle. I was relieved to be spared from that task, as I was always afraid I'd spear some poor animal with a pitchfork.

Getting silage down from the silos was another chore I was assigned. Ralph had made a two wheeled cart that would just fit through the door behind the horses and the door to the landing at the side of the silo. I pulled the cart behind me through the two doors, remembering to speak to the horses as I passed behind them. The other way to move the cart into position was to push it into place, but that required me to climb over the cart to get to the silo itself.

The next step was to clamber up and into the silo, carrying a pitchfork, using the silo's hoops like rungs of a ladder until I reached the top of the remaining silage. "We" had made a chute for each silo about three feet by four feet, extending from the level of the main barn floor up to near the top of the silo.

The view from the top of the silo was always impressive unless, of course, it was raining or snowing! From the top of the silo, above the roofs of the barn and applehouse, I could gaze at the winter night sky and marvel at the billions of stars twinkling above. Most often it was very still. Once in a while I could hear the muffled sounds of the chores being done a world away on the floor of the barn. And if the moon was out, I could see everything now bathed in a pale blue.

I may have gazed and dreamed for quite a while one night, until Pres hollered up, "Hey, you fall asleep up there?"

There was very little light in the silo. Most of the time I used a flashlight (if I remembered to bring one with me) or depended on the dim star- or moonlight. I then dug out forkfuls of silage and tossed them down the chute into the cart below. If my star-gazing reverie had been too long, the horses would forget I had recently passed them. That first fork-full, dropping twenty feet or more with a solid "Foomp" into the silage cart would startle the tar out of them. I must admit that I took a kind of perverse pleasure at their reaction, those dastardly manure machines whose excrement I had earlier cleaned up!

During the dead of winter, the silage would begin to freeze, despite the heat of the slow oxidation. The top would freeze to a depth of a couple of inches or so between feedings, and often, during a prolonged cold snap, I would need a pick or an adze to break out the first forkfuls. The silage would also freeze to the sides of the silo as well. During a real long cold spell, the inside of the silo would look pretty hairy.

Many people find the smell of silage to be objectionable. I always liked the pungently sweet smell of silage. It's a smell that reflects successful, controlled fermentation, one that I've come to recognize - and appreciate - in many adult beverages.

The bottom of the older, first silo was six or eight feet below the level of the barn floor. That meant that toward the end of emptying the contents of the silo, I had to pitch the silage UP to get it into the cart! I quickly learned that it was easier to leave the cart outside and pitch the silage onto the floor of the chute, then from there, into the cart. The newer, second silo's bottom was only a foot or so below the level of the barn floor, so it was not a problem.

Hauling maple sap from Smith Hill back to the farm, about 1945. Pres is the driver. Others are unknown. Dog is Scarlet. Apple Valley Road wouldn't be paved for another couple of years.
Dorothy N. Townsley photo, Author's Collection.

We made maple syrup and maple sugar at the farm until Fred died. I say, "we," but I was only ten when he died, so I know I was probably more nuisance than help. The sugaring season began with tapping the maple trees. We hoped to have this phase finished by the time the days became long enough and the sun bright enough to warm the daytime temperatures over freezing - freezing nights and warm days work like a pump to move the maple sap up toward the budding leaves.

Pres fixed up a logging sled with a huge tin tub on it. He'd drive the team up into the maple orchard. For gathering sap on Smith Hill, where we tapped trees on both sides of road, Pres and Ralph mounted two big tin tubs on a wheeled wagon. Usually there was another man or two who went from tree to tree emptying the spigot-hung buckets into large gathering pails which were then dumped into the tubs on the sled.

Sometimes I'd be sent to look into the buckets to see if they held any sap (sometimes, depending on the day or the setting or some other reason, there was little or no sap in the bucket). If there wasn't, I'd saved somebody from having to go to that bucket. There were occasional surprises in the buckets.

The buckets were covered, so most falling forest debris was avoided, but after a storm there might be some twigs and pieces of bark floating in the sap. It was common to find a variety of moths, and once we found a tiny drowned mouse that had somehow clambered to the rim of the bucket and fallen in.

The Sugarhouse, in operation, about 1986. Roland, Fred's grandson is at the arch, magician-du-saison.
Betsey W. Lyman Photo.

Fred, Pres and Ralph's father, did all the boiling down of the sap. The sugar house, where this was done, was the farthest building from the farmhouse. I had to take Fred a thermos of coffee once in a while. It was a long walk in the March snow and wind past the icehouse and the woodshed. Often it was pretty dark out as well, which added a hint of pending danger to it. I was glad to get to the door of the sugar house because it was always warm inside, with the slab-fired arch door open and the sparks darting about as Fred chucked more wood under the boiling pans. Always the sweet smelling steam swirled above the pans and sometimes around Fred as he sat in the corner. Fred never said much. I was afraid of him, or perhaps in awe of him, this larger-than-life magician who coaxed the sweet sap to become syrup.

We used syrup as our sweetener – on cereal in the morning, in coffee. We had to buy granulated sugar, which during the war years was rationed, so it was hard to find it anywhere at any price. But we had plenty of maple syrup and maple sugar. One real big treat was putting maple syrup on homemade ice cream. Lillian Williams would mound up soup bowls of homemade vanilla ice cream for Russ and me, then pour a liberal amount of maple syrup atop it – so much that you had to eat quickly to keep it from overflowing onto the table.

Several holidays broke up the oppressive monotony of winter. As a youngster Christmas was my favorite holiday, probably because of all the presents!

I have just an impression, not really a memory, of Mother holding me in her arms so I could reach out and ever-so-gently ding the little glass Christmas bell ornament on the tree on Christmas morning. I can still see the tinsel on the tree sparkling in the early morning sun, and I can still smell the fragrance of the tree.

During the year, as Pres worked in the woods, he would spot candidates for the year's Christmas tree. A couple of weeks before Christmas, he, Shirley and I would trudge off to wherever, cut down the tree, and drag it back to the house. Often the tree came from the Brown lot tree nursery, from which Pres would wholesale Christmas trees when he could.

Usually we would set it up right away in the living room, its butt in a coffee can, which in turn, was anchored in the vee of an old steel plow point. Sometimes we'd discretely tie a couple of pieces of string to the nearby window casings. The tree had to be pretty stable, as Peter, Lucky and Rainbow, our house cats, found the tree to be a great place to climb and explore. Brucie, the Cocker Spaniel, was more reserved, only sniffing it from time to time. I barely remember the tree coming down once from cat depredations. I'm told that I did the tree considerable damage one time where I was angry at Mother and threw my boot into the decorated tree.

Shirley and I were in charge of decorating the tree, and we'd make a project of it. I barely remember the time Mother refers to when the tree was heavily decorated from about mid-tree down, the limits of Shirley's and my reach. Mom would discreetly rearrange the decorations after we had gone to bed, to get a better balance (both physically and aesthetically).

Mother would put the lights on the tree first, then she would turn Shirley and me loose. Most of the decorations were blown glass in various colors.

I was especially impressed with half a dozen good-sized red ones which had stars etched on the sides. And my favorite was that light colored blown glass bell I mentioned earlier, the one with a tiny clapper that made the most beautiful tinkling sound when I was allowed to ever so gently reach out and lightly nudge it.

I fervently believed in Santa Claus and his eight tiny reindeer. Rudolph came along in the late 1940s, after my imagination had been replaced with reality. On Christmas Eve, Shirley and I would drape a pair of Pres' work socks on the couch in the living room. His size twelves could hold so many more presents than our kid size socks. We could open them as soon as we got up. The regular exchange of presents took place after breakfast.

Nannie and Gramp usually had a small, table-top tree. I felt bad for them then, but I can understand now: the real meaning of Christmas in not in the beauty of the tree or the mound of presents beneath it, but in the wonder in children's eyes, the love the season inspires, and the hope and the promise for countless happy holidays to come.

Though it's hard to pick a "best ever" Christmas present, one might have been the Christmas I received Tinker Toys as a present. I can still smell the fresh, new right-out-of-the-box wood smell. Another "best" may have been the Christmas I got a Lincoln Logs set – I can remember the smell of them, too, as they were stained. I hated to get clothes. They were a terrible waste of Christmas money that could be far better spent on toys and models!

New Year's Eve was just another night to us kids at the farm. I don't recall Mother and Pres ever going out to celebrate.

President Lincoln, and to a lesser extent, President Washington, fascinated me. I read voraciously everything Lincoln I could find. I was just a little miffed that nobody was excited enough to celebrate the birthday of this very important man. At least we sort of celebrated George Washington's Birthday, though it most often fell in the middle of February school vacation, so it was almost invisible.

For Valentines Day some of the mothers made cupcakes for us to take to school. You were required to send a valentine to every kid in the class. I hated it.

Shirley and I played the usual Monopoly and Parcheesi and Chinese Checkers. Nannie was a great hand to entertain her grandchildren with card games. One was a wild and wooly (but easily understood) version of Rummy, in which runs could be pieced together in any collection of suits. She also taught us to play "Steal the Old Man's Bundle," whose rules I'd forgotten – but I just found them on the Internet - so I can pass it on to my grandchildren.

Pres taught Bill Townsley and me to play Cribbage as early teenagers, and later Mother and Pres taught Shirley and me to play Pitch.

Although radio was the main regular contact we had with the world outside of Ashfield, we got a daily newspaper. The Greenfield *Recorder-Gazette* arrived by mail and was therefore at least a day late. Still, the comics were good, and it was here I developed my life-long habit of reading the headlines, then the sports, and finally the comics. Fred and Grammie got the Springfield *Republican* on Sundays. Its comics took up a whole section – and they were in color! There were Prince Valiant and Alley Oop and Mark Trail's outdoor strip, and Pogo and L'il Abner.

Radio was on all day, though its format was wholly different from today's. For one, most of our news we learned through radio. We listened to the news from Greenfield on WHAI. We listened to Bob Steele in the morning on WTIC out of Hartford. We sometimes listened to WBZ from Boston. Don Kent's weather forecasts could be depended upon, given a little country windage for the hundred miles in distance and the thousand feet in altitude.

We developed favorites, of course. For me, the most favorite has to be "The Lone Ranger." Mine was the second generation to be dazzled by the strains of *The William Tell Overture*. It was probably the first piece of classical music I'd heard. It was a surprise to find later that the part we heard on Lone Ranger was just the end of a much longer piece of music.

There was a magic to radio drama shows. Through the gift of the show's sound effects we could hear the crackling of the small campfire. But through the gift of imagination we could smell the mesquite smoke, and we could see the faces of the Lone Ranger and Tonto in the flickering light of the campfire. When the episode came to an end, we could imagine seeing the village sheriff as he looked at the silver bullet and wondered aloud, "Who was the masked man?" As we heard in the distance the hearty "Hi-yo, Silver! Away!" we could nod knowingly to one another, confident that once again, the Lone Ranger and Tonto had triumphed over evil!

The Lone Ranger was on three nights a week at 7:30. We raced through getting ready for bed, so that we could listen raptly for the half hour show. Funny, I can't remember what was on Tuesdays or Thursdays.

Another hour of favorites occurred every weekday late afternoon from 5 pm to 6. This was the realm of "Straight Arrow," "Sergeant Preston of the Yukon," "Tom Mix," "Clyde Beatty" and several others. We raced through the barn chores to make sure we could be in front of the radio by 5 pm.

Still another hour or so of favorites was on Sunday evenings. Here were "Our Miss Brooks," "Jack Benny," "Amos and Andy" and others. As we grew older, we learned there were a number of radio serials on after Lone Ranger. "The Shadow" lurked here, and "The Green Hornet," with his faithful valet,

Cato. "Gunsmoke" debuted as an evening radio show, originally with William Conrad in the role that James Arness would make famous.

The first television I remember seeing was at the home of Bill's grandmother Craft (Dr. Craft's widow). She was watching "I Remember Mama" when Clayton, Bill and I stopped in. I was perhaps 11 or 12. Bill's across-the-street neighbor had a TV, and she regularly invited the neighborhood kids in to watch "Howdy Doody." Not too long after that, Bill's mom and dad got a television, and invited the Townsleys and the LaBelles, I think, to watch "Ed Sullivan."

Television came to the farm in the summer of 1954. Floyd and Jane Townsley and their kids, Bill, Ginnie and Lynn were visiting. Floyd wanted to watch the hearing that Senator Joseph McCarthy was conducting looking for Communists in the Army.

Floyd had bought a TV and an antenna. The table model round-tube (I think) TV was in the sitting room. The antenna was on the hill, maybe two hundred feet away, beside the pear trees. He constructed a home-made lead-in consisting of two single copper wires separated every three or four inches by a quarter-inch diameter, inch-long white plastic spreader. You'd heat the wire with a blow torch and quickly apply the tube end to it so the wire would melt down into the plastic.

Aiming the antenna was a never-ending task, because the slightest breeze turned it in a new direction. Floyd climbed one of the pear trees to reach the antenna, and Jane would shout to him. Any time the wind blew, some of the spreaders would pop off, eventually shorting out the antenna altogether. The lead-in would ice up in a freezing drizzle, and over time would begin to short out the antenna. Grammie asked me once to see if I could improve reception by knocking the ice off the lead-in. I succeeded in knocking off a little ice and a lot of spreaders, eventually shorting out the antenna.

We sometimes watched TV downstairs at Grammie Townsley's. "I Married Joan," a comedy starring Joan Blondell, was fun, as was "Mr. Peepers" with Wally Cox, and William Bendix in "Life of Riley."

We didn't have a TV of our own upstairs until about 1956.

Once in a while we were fortunate enough to find somebody courageous enough to take us to the movies, in Greenfield either at the Garden or the Vic (Victoria) or perhaps the Lawlor.

I liked adventure films. "Moby Dick," with Gregory Peck as Captain Ahab made a lasting impression, as did "Caine Mutiny," with Humphrey Bogart as Captain Queeg. If we went to the movies with Gramp and Nannie, as we sometimes did, they'd prefer a "Ma and Pa Kettle" movie (Marjory Main and Percy Kilbride) which was always rollicking good fun.

"Greatest Show On Earth," with Charlton Heston, is one early movie I remember. I recall bits and pieces of others, but I can't put them in any order. There was "Song of the South" ("Zippety-do-dah, zippety-yay"). There was once a "coming attractions" that scared the daylights out of me. It was for a gangster movie, I assume, and the snippet I can still clearly see today, was slow-motion of a guy getting shot in the hand. I still see the skin peeling back from the blast. Among my favorite actors were Gregory Peck and Charlton Heston, noted above, and also Gary Cooper and John Wayne. They were all the strong, reserved, confident heroes I'd like to become.

Winter slowly drains into Spring. The first very faint hints that winter may be finite come perhaps in mid-January, when the days become just a little bit longer. Most years there's a January thaw. By early March the temperatures begin to creep up toward the forties, prompting a frenzy of activity to tap the maple trees. Although there may be one or two humdinger snowstorms after the first of March (the infamous "Blizzard of [18]88" was around March 20), snow has begun to melt, and by early April is down to a few patches of dirty stuff – not at all as picturesque as when it first fell back in January.

Chapter 8
Spring

Spring arrives quietly one evening in mid to late March in Ashfield with the plaintive peep of a single spring peeper. The tiny tree frog's solo is soon joined by thousands of his brothers and sisters. Before long, the symphony of spring is swelled by returning robins, phoebes and barn swallows and the shrill whistles of woodchucks as they emerge from hibernation. Signs of winter still abound - in patches of dirty snow, moldy grass and muddy barnyards, but spring's pervasive air of hope and expectancy firmly sweeps away winter's despair. Everything is new again; God has given us a fresh start.

I'm an unabashed fan of spring! It is my favorite time of the year, in spite of the pesky black flies and pollen-laden air. I've liked spring, ever since I was a child. One spring I was so anxious to play baseball that I shoveled the snow off the front lawn in late February.

For several years Mother set up a small aquarium with frog eggs. There was a small pool just below the bridge, more a stagnant drainage pool than anything else, and each spring there was a new crop of frog eggs. Frogs lay eggs by the zillion. Each egg is essentially a small black dot of life in a sphere of clear yolk (there are no shells, as there are with bird eggs). The edges of that tiny backwater were a mass of gelatinous goop. Mother scooped perhaps a couple of quarts of frog eggs and placed them in a five gallon aquarium, filling it the rest of the way with spring water.

Shirley and I watched eagerly at first for the earliest sign of newly hatched polliwogs. Some people call them tadpoles, but we knew them as polliwogs. After a while the newness wore off, and several days might go by before we discovered that there were dozens of them squiggling around! We watched the polliwogs well into the summer as they grew legs and lost their tails, until one day Mother "returned them to nature" – that is, flushed them down the toilet. In those days, flushing them down the toilet was not necessarily the sentence of death it now would be, as the farmhouse wastewater system drained directly into the brook above the bridge.

We boys anxiously awaited the beginning of the trout fishing season, for many years the 15th of April. We had begun looking forward to opening day late in the Fall and were feverish by the appointed day. For several weeks now the fishing pole had been dusted off; the reel taken apart, wiped off, reassembled and well-oiled; last year's line stripped off and replaced with new. Eagle Claw fish hooks with leaders on them are sold, a half dozen to a "folder," and we received several folders for Christmas and birthdays. Lead split shot sinkers have been carefully clipped to the line just above the leaders. A can of earthworms, the fattest and juiciest, have been dug and placed, with just the right amount of dirt, in an old tin band-aide box or a soup tin.

The night before opening day, we had trouble getting to sleep. Visions of monster rainbow trout ran through our heads. All the same, we worried about what could go wrong. What *could* go wrong??

Possibly the ground was still frozen so we couldn't dig up any worms.

Possibly the brook was still iced over and Mother wouldn't think it was safe enough.

Possibly it would rain and our fingers would be too cold to bait the hook.

Possibly it would *snow* – even worse than rain!

Possibly there would be too many fishermen.

Having opening day of the fishing season on a Saturday was a mixed blessing. You could fish all day, but all those *old* guys who worked at Lamson-Goodnow, Greenfield Tap and Die, Kendall Mills and other factories would be out there, too. It didn't seem fair to us that even though we had carefully scouted where all the biggest trout were, those *old* guys might just catch them before we could get there!

But having opening day on a weekday was a problem, too, unless magically it was during April school vacation. Otherwise we had to get up early so we could be home in time for the school bus.

For all the hoopla and planning and anticipation, most opening days resulted in just a few fish before we got cold or bored.

Spring brings many seasonal tasks. One such task for apple growers like us was picking up the brush from where Pres had pruned the apple trees during the winter.

Pruning is done during the winter and early spring. The main object is to open the tree up so that sunlight can reach the apples as they develop during the summer. Pruning is more an art form than science, requiring wisdom and judgment – and a little guesswork and luck. I tried several times but Pres was never satisfied with what I did. Pres wasn't much of a teacher – he knew his job but couldn't explain it, so most of what I learned was from watching him.

During the infrequent in-between-other-work times, Pres headed for the orchard to prune the apple trees. Most of the time he used hand clippers and a small pruning saw (which I inherited and still use today) and an apple-picking ladder. He'd work down a row of trees leaving a trail of branches and twigs underneath each tree.

When most of the snow was melted, it was time to pick up the apple brush and burn it. Pres harnessed the team of horses to a logging sled and laid a light wooden framework on the sled, something he - or more likely Ralph – had cobbled up especially for this task. We would drive up and down the paths between the trees, and when we had a sled-load, Pres drove it back to the upper of two stone bridges which spanned the small brook that bisected the orchard. There we rolled the brush off the sled and over the lower side of the bridge. When enough had accumulated below the bridge, Pres set the pile afire.

Burning the brush was always an adventure. It was still pretty "green" (firewood needs to be dried for a couple of months at least before it will burn well), so we used kerosene, old used motor oil, or (if you were foolhardy) a little gasoline. We also built the pile of brush on one or more old car or truck tires. The result, hopefully, was a roaring blaze, which began, with the motor oil and the burning tires, as a thick black smoke. Each time at least one of the fire towers in the area would call the farm to find out if there was a problem.

The apple growing cycle begins again in earnest in early May. You could argue it never ended, and that's the thing about cycles. Early in May, Pres brought the apple spraying and dusting equipment out of storage. The key is the emergence of apple buds, which awakens some wee bugs that love to munch on apple blossoms. From then on, Pres carried on a war with apple parasites until the apples were about ready to be picked in September.

Spraying involved mixing chemicals with water. Pres usually drew the water from a little pool in the stream that came down though the orchard. He had a small gasoline powered pump to pull the water out of the pool, and he was forever having problems! All thumbs when it came to machinery, he often failed to get the pump started – and never failed to get wildly frustrated in the process. Often, late in the season, there was precious little water in the tiny brook to be of use.

Though spraying had to be done according to a schedule, it could be done any time of the day, as long as the spray had time enough to dry on the apples. A major problem was the weather: sometimes it seemed you'd only just get the spray on the apples when along came a shower to wash it all off! By the 1950s spraying technology required two men to apply the spray. Pres and Richard Clark partnered, spraying both Clark's and Townsley's orchards in a one or two session application.

Pres, dusting apple trees early in the season in the late 1950s. Despite the absence of masks and other breathing protection, neither he nor the horses ever had respiratory problems!
Dorothy N. Townsley Photo, Author's Collection.

Dusting, too, had to be done to a schedule of what bugs emerge at what time of the season, but dusting was most often done early in the morning so it would stick to the dew on the apples and there dry to finish the process.

As I look back on the process, I wonder that Pres never had any respiratory or skin problems. He never used any particular protection, neither for himself nor for his horses, and he lived to be nearly ninety!

With the arrival of spring comes a host of urgent tasks. One early spring task – or perhaps even late winter – is spreading manure. The idea is to dig out the accumulated animal waste from the manure pit – that dark, dank and smelly "basement" of the barn we visited in Chapter 2 - and spread it on the fields as fertilizer. We used two implements, a manure spreader and one or more tractors - one with a front end loader to dig out the manure and a second one to pull the spreader.

Manure spreaders are wonders of mechanical engineering. Basically they are wagons with a two-part mechanism to dispense manure over the ground as widely and evenly as possible. One part of the mechanism pulls the manure apart and "kicks" it out of the wagon onto the field; the other part conveys the wagonload to the kicker mechanism. Working properly, it rattles and clatters and manure flies off at a merry rate – it's a marvel to see and hear, especially for a youngster!

There are two ways to power the mechanism. One is to use the spreader's wheels to drive the conveyor and the "kicker," in the same principle as the old push-type reel lawn mowers. Although it's efficient, it does not work well in a field that is wet: the wheels can skid over wet ground, sometimes without turning at all.

The other way to power a manure spreader is by taking the power from the tractor. The spreader wheels thus may turn freely without having to drive the mechanism.

Spreading manure is not a thing to do on a windy day – sometimes the wind can catch the flying manure and blow it back over the tractor - and over its driver. All the fields, whether they are hayfields or cornfields or gardens, get fertilizer.

Preparing the cornfields and gardens for planting is another of the regular seasonal tasks. With plowing, the object is literally to turn the sod over, so the grass or whatever was planted there the year before - and the fertilizer we just spread - lies face down and the dirt is up facing the sun. Modern plows, typically, are one or more heavy, curved steel blades. Each blade has a hardened steel point firmly riveted to it. The point is designed so it breaks off if you hit some underground obstruction, like a large boulder, of which there is a never-ending supply in our part of New England. Plow blades are "ganged" (joined) together; obviously you'd like to have as many ganged together as possible. The right number is governed by the power of whatever is pulling the plow, and by the coarseness of the soil.

We used a variety of plows while I was growing up. For gardens, Pres sometimes used a single gang plow with two handles, to which he hitched a single horse. He tied the ends of the reins together and looped them over his shoulders, wrestled the plow into position (even a single gang plow is heavy!). With a chirp to the horse, off he went, alternately steering the horse in a straight line and adjusting the plow depth and direction with the handles. It was grueling hard work!

Pres did most of the plowing behind his team of horses using a two-ganged plow. The horse-drawn plow was a two-wheeled, sit-upon mechanism. The plow blades could be raised and lowered via a ratcheted handle near the seat.

Ralph, Malcolm, and almost everyone else plowed using a tractor, and this was how I learned. I especially liked Malcolm's blue Ford tractor – it didn't have power steering, which meant I could put the left front tire in the furrow of the last pass and keep it there with slight rightward pressure on the steering wheel while I watched the plow for problems.

Plowing was the first step in preparing the fields. For most of us Yankee hill farmers, the next step is "picking stone," and for me this was the chore I disliked the most!

Here's a little background for those of you who aren't familiar with removing rocks, stones, boulders and stumps from newly cleared land or a plowed field. There are many steps to clearing land, especially in New England. Most of the steps are one-time-only, like cutting the trees, clearing the brush, removing the stumps. Though hard to do, these are satisfying tasks, because you can see sometimes significant progress at the end of the project. You know these steps won't have to be done again. Plowing must be done each year, but I never found this offensive, perhaps because I always did it using a tractor.

But picking stone - oh mercy! Year after year, there was always a new crop of stones that the freezing and thawing cycle had raised toward the surface. No matter how thoroughly you went over a piece of land, there was always the promise of more backbreaking hard work next year! Ralph always told me it was "character-building," but there came a point when I felt my character was built well enough!

I was, and still am, thoroughly frustrated by jobs like picking stone – what do I have to show, six months later, for all the hard labor I've expended? And even today as I mow the lawn, or rake leaves, or shovel snow, I think about Ralph and building character.

Picking stone was followed by harrowing. There are at least two kinds of harrows. A disc harrow had several rows of dish-shaped foot wide discs, which, when pulled by a tractor or team of horses across the garden or field, broke the dirt clods into finer pieces. A tooth harrow accomplished the same thing using a lattice frame to which many six-inch long steel teeth were affixed.

We always had a sizeable garden which had to be planted by Memorial Day – it was disgraceful to plant anything later than that. Many years we embarrassed ourselves by planting well into June. Everything had to be planted in straight rows. We stretched a piece of string between a couple of pegs and tried to follow it as closely as possible as we planted the seeds.

The first thing in was peas, as they could stand a brief overnight frost. Peas were planted along the row, and later we put up a length of chicken wire fence for the peas to climb on. Radishes went in about the same time, as they grew better in the cooler early part of summer. We planted corn (in groups of four or five seed kernels spaced about a foot apart), then string beans and shell beans (planted about like the corn). There were pumpkins, summer squash, winter squash, each planted in hills several feet apart. We planted beets, carrots, parsnips, turnips. For the life of me I never understood why anyone would actually plant anything as gag-inducing as turnip. The only answer I ever heard was, "Pres likes turnip," which, I guess, was good enough. We planted leafy lettuce and cabbages. We bought seedling tomatoes from Eastern States Farmers Exchange in the railroad yard at Shelburne Falls – now Agway along Route 2. In addition, Mother made sure there was a sizeable row of gladiolas and another of zinnias.

For many years while we lived at the farm, Mother had a flower garden right next to the vegetable garden. There was a fence around it, mostly to keep marauding cattle out of it. Most of the flowers' names I've forgotten, but I remember some hollyhocks and peonies. And "sweet william" – the name sounded weird to this youngster, as none of the Williams I knew could be called "sweet!"

There were lots of pansies in the flower garden. On Mother's Day the Sunday School sent us home with a pansy in a small container. We kids helped plant them in the garden. We checked on our special pansy several times a day at first, but after it produced pickable flowers to bring Mother, interest waned.

There also were seemingly thousands of johnny-jump-ups[16]. A cousin of the pansies – johnny-jump-up blossoms indeed look like miniature pansy. Johnny-jump-ups are a hardy lot; pansies don't usually reproduce themselves, but johnny-jump-ups spread like fury. We looked at johnny-jump-ups as weeds, and any time we were dispatched to the garden with a tool, we were to hack out those pesky johnny-jump-ups.

Thinning out the planted vegetables and just general weeding was the next job. Some of those seeds were incredibly small, making it difficult to put down an evenly spaced row of seeds. If left to nature, carrots and beets and stuff would all come up in clumps, too close together to grow nice and fat like you'd like to have them. Your job would be to select those that would grow big and robust, and pull up the rest.

Simple and straight forward, right?

Of course not! Do you know how alike seedling carrots and seedling field grass could be? How alike newly emerged lettuce leaves and plantain were? For a few days after they emerged, veggies and weeds grow side by side, but as time goes on, it became easier to spot which was which – the weeds were bigger and more robust than any of the vegetables!

---

16 Johnny-jump-ups are called "violas" in some parts of the country, I learned recently.

A simple garden hoe soon became the main weapon of choice in the war on weeds. I preferred a hoe with a fairly narrow blade. It was sharp enough to slice off the weed tops, yet wide enough to push dirt around to smother the weeds.

Though I never asked at the time, there was a reason for planting things in straight rows: it made it easier to cultivate (to loosen the soil to expose the roots of the weeds to air and sunlight – which would kill them). Every week or two, depending on how the weeds were growing, Pres would hitch one of the horses to a cultivator. The horse-drawn cultivator was a fairly simple device: a heavy piece of oak, perhaps a 4" x 4" about three feet long, to which was attached an interchangeable set of tines/teeth, and two handles by which you held the cultivator upright and guided it as the horse pulled it between the rows of vegetables.

Cultivating the garden, about 1948. Pres at the cultivator, Shirley seated on Chub,
Fabian Stone, with his beagle, leads Chub through the corn.
Dorothy N. Townsley Photo, Author's Collection.

The horse pulled the cultivator between the rows while you guided the cultivator to attack the weeds. You tied the reins together and looped them over your shoulders, you picked up the cultivator and wrestled it to about where you wanted to begin, then you "Giddap" the horse.

Another nice, simple, straight-forward labor-saving process, right?

First, your horse has very little concept of "straight" - except when he's headed toward the barn! Second, your horse cannot differentiate between "weeds" and "vegetables" (to him its all green stuff that ought to be eaten), and would as soon step on one as the other. It takes two hands to pull those reins which you looped over your shoulders to steer the horse left or right, those same two hands you're using to hold the cultivator upright and guide it between the rows. The whole process is fraught with variables, any combination of which could raise the level of shouting (you horse-savvy folks know that does not improve the horse's performance!).

The alternative to the horse-drawn cultivator was a much lighter, much more maneuverable hand cultivator. It was essentially a lighter weight version of the horse-drawn cultivator, except it had a big wheel in front. Instead of the horse pulling it, you pushed the cultivator between the rows. As I got older and physically big enough to push a hand cultivator, it was most often my job. The position became mine because I was the youngest physically capable male who wasn't smart enough yet to dodge the assignment.

Pres owned a wood lot atop the hill behind "the Brown place" and along Cemetery Road in Buckland. In the late 1950s a pair of beavers had settled in and built a dam across the drainage from a small swamp. The placement of the dam was pretty ingenious: there was a low area shaped like a shallow pitcher, and the beavers had constructed their dam across the spout. With a dam of less than three feet in height by twenty feet long, the beavers created a pool of perhaps three acres.

Now ordinarily the Townsleys are appreciative of the wonders of nature, and can admire God's work in a stand of graceful hemlocks and in the patience and focus of beavers as they create marvelous ponds. But when those graceful hemlocks happened to be in the middle of that marvelous pond, the Townsleys were something less than appreciative. The problem is that hemlocks (and most other forest trees) will die if their roots remain under water for long. Dead trees soon begin to rot, and rotted trees make lousy lumber.

So one fine May Sunday morning in 1958, Ralph, Pres and I planted six half sticks of dynamite across the dam and with an authoritative *Whump!!!*, blew it to smithereens.

After the quick shower of sticks and mud and water ended, we could see that the dam had been heavily damaged and water was gushing through the hole. Where there had been a trickle flowing down the hill toward High Street in Buckland, there now was a torrent crashing and tumbling down the hillside. Moments later, two fishermen ran for their lives from the incredible, inexplicable flash flood. Still later, a small footbridge was quickly swept away downstream.

Ralph, Pres and I stood on what little was left of the dam and watched, satisfied, as the water level above the dam slowly began to drop. But before long, as we wordlessly gathered our tools for the trek home, Ralph got my attention and pointed a ways up the pond where two "vees" on the water surface slowly approached the dam. Two intrepid beavers, submerged except for their noses and eyeballs, swam up to see what was causing their protective water level to drop.

Later that the afternoon I saddled Lady, Shirley's grey mare, grabbed my .22, and rode the three miles or so from the farm to the dam to see if I could shoot some beavers which must, by then, have been trying to repair the dam. I tied her to a bush nearest the dam and walked down over the ledges to the dam, but there were no beavers to be seen. I about scared the mare to death as I thrashed back out of the brush. I always wondered if she thought I was a bear, or if she had smelled a bear in the area. It was a quick trip back down the hill to the farm!

To finish the story, the beavers ended up winning the battle: in a couple of weeks they had the dam back to nearly its pre-blast level. The following winter, after the ice was thick enough to hold his team of horses, Pres logged off all the saleable lumber. The following spring, the Valiton brothers stocked the pond with several bullheads (catfish) which multiplied lustily and provided fun fishing for all who could find the remote pond.

Gramp Nelson was caretaker of the Ashfield cemeteries for a few years. I helped him rake leaves, etc., each spring. During the summers, I'd help mow the cemeteries. He used a big three gang reel power mower to do the main areas, and I used a smaller rotary power mower to get from where he left off up to the headstones. I'd finish off with hand grass clippers. I got 75 cents an hour. I was amazed to learn how many cemeteries there were in Ashfield. Besides the big Plain Cemetery on Baptist Corner Road, there was the Hill Cemetery, not far from the golf course. There were smaller plots in Baptist Corner. One was supposed to be haunted by somebody who had been hanged from a big oak tree that stood nearby. There were still others in Spruce Corner and South Ashfield. I never got to the Northwest Cemetery on top of Pumpkin Hill in Apple Valley.

After a spate of holidays in the late Fall and early Winter, there was little relief from the rhythm of school. Somehow, the fact that we had a week's vacation in February and another in April didn't work into the equation; it was just a bummer not to have a day-off-holiday in the Spring.

St. Patrick's Day as a youth was nothing special, except that it was very close to Bill Craft's and Joe LaBelle's birthdays. Bill Craft's family always wore green - his Grandmother Jenny Johnston was Irish.

Of all the Christian holidays, Easter is my favorite. It wasn't always so; I was easily swayed by Christmas as a youngster. But the glory and glitter of Christmas has tarnished as I've grown older. The wonder and mystery of Christ's birth have been smothered by commercialism, and anything meaningful has been lost in the insane plunge from soon after Halloween to Christmas morning. Easter still keeps some of its luster, even though it, too, is crowded with colorful bunnies that hatch eggs.

Today, I believe Easter is the holiest and most important of our Christian holy days. It's not the birth of Jesus, but his death and miraculous resurrection that make Christianity a viable important religion.

Easter was celebrated with a family dinner - at Nannie and Gramp's, and later at my folks at the schoolhouse. Grammie Townsley was usually included, as was Aunt Floss Greenman and whomever of her kids was around. Aunt Martha and Uncle Ralph, with Russell and later, Roland, joined us sometimes.

Shirley says I really fooled her one year for April Fools Day, though I can't remember it. She says I led her to believe that I had built her a lily pond in the side hill pasture above the sugar house. She says I never actually said I made one, but I certainly never denied it either.

One time when I was five or six, Nannie had me make a May Basket for Gramp Nelson. We made it out of strips of colored paper woven together. We picked some flowers, pansies, I think, or forget-me-nots or violets. Dogtooth violets were sometimes available. Even at six, it seemed kind of silly.

Mothers Day was usually the occasion for another family dinner, most often at our house. Nannie and Gramp were usually there, as were Grammie Townsley, and sometimes Aunt Floss Greenman and her kids were around. Some years it was warm enough to have the get together on the front lawn.

Memorial Day in Ashfield was sort of an "old home day" for the grownups, so there was quite a gathering. We spent a whole chapter there earlier, so there's no more to be added.

Chapter 9
School Days

Formal schooling began for me in September, 1947. I was six years old, nearly seven. There was no kindergarten or pre-school in Ashfield until much later.

The school year in Ashfield began a day or two after Labor Day. The only remarkable thing in our school year was that classes were suspended, right after they started, for Greenfield Fair, at first for Wednesday, Thursday and Friday, then later just for Wednesday. Other than that, it was Labor Day to mid June, with a week or more off at Christmas, another week in February and yet another in April. There were occasional planned holidays, like Thanksgiving and Easter, when Easter didn't fall during the April vacation.

I went to the Ashfield Consolidated School for grades 1 through 8, then Sanderson Academy, from which I graduated in June, 1959. All twelve grades were housed together in one big building on Buckland Road in Ashfield.

I got to school by bus all twelve years. I have a faint impression of seeing a green school bus coming into view as it came down Apple Valley Road that first day of school in 1947.

Our bus most often was driven by Helen Ward. One day she must have been daydreaming or something as she drove right on past the stop at the Townsley farm, finally dropping me off at Nannie and Gramp's - with profuse apologies. Every day for weeks after that, as we rounded the curve above the farm, I felt obligated to quietly whisper in her ear, "Townsley stop…" A very few times, when the bus was out of service for maintenance, Mrs. Ward would do the bus route in her Cadillac. Hers was the first air-conditioned car I ever rode in.

As a youngster I read only when I was so forced or coerced, and it was only as I got older that I began to enjoy reading. I liked "*The Little Engine that Could*" (the Watty Piper one) when Mother read it to me as bedtime story, and later when I could read it myself. The Thornton Burgess "*Mother West Wind*" series that included "*Lightfoot, the Deer*" and others were early favorites. In high school, I read Hemingway's "*Old Man and the Sea*" for a book report and was dazzled by it.

I read if I had to, but I loved comic books! My favorites were *Straight Arrow* and *The Lone Ranger*, and I tried hard to get the latest monthly issues at Sawyer's in Shelburne Falls. *Superman* and others were acceptable, but my two western heroes, *Lone Ranger* and *Straight Arrow*, were tops! Later on, when I could get them, the Classics series, comic book adaptations of literary classics, provided excellent material for book reports. It sort of felt like cheating, and I felt just a little guilty doing it, but it didn't stop me.

Socially, I had few problems. I adjusted to having glasses (since about second grade), and survived being called "four eyes" for a time. Dealing with emerging adolescence at a time when my self confidence was low was difficult, as it was for many, I learned later.

Lasting friendships are often formed in grade school, and three of us, Russ Williams, Bill Craft and I, have remained close over the years since.

Russell, a neighbor up the road in Ashfield, and I had played together even before we began school.

During grade school, Bill and I became close friends. We often slept over at one another's homes. Mother and Ruth, Bill's mom, sometimes arranged a trade: I would go to Craft's and Sue, Bill's sister, would visit Shirley at our house – or the other way around.

Our typical school day outfit was as follows: dark sox (Mother knit me a nice pair of argyles once), jockey shorts and a strapped undershirt. Everyone wore low cut brown or black leather shoes. The only sneakers available were the high-top ones, and you wore them only for gym. Jeans were the usual pants, but as we grew older, chinos became the pants of choice. Everyone wore a collared shirt, usually long-sleeved.

During the cooler weather, which is most of the time in New England, we needed a fall jacket or winter coat. I had a nice warm sheepskin coat one winter when I was about 12. I was really sad to outgrow it. Some kids of necessity wore hand-me-downs, but I don't remember having to wear anything like that - either that, or I was so traumatized that I've suppressed the memory of it.

When it rained or snowed, we wore a raincoat over our regular coat, and black rubber buckle boots. Those awful buckle boots – the buckles would ice up as you played in the snow, and sometimes you'd have to wait a few minutes in the indoor warmth to unbuckle them.

Speaking of boots and such – once in a while during the winter we had a glorious snow day! With the first flakes of snow, indeed with even the *forecast* of snow, began a universal ritual. If the forecast was the least bit questionable, Shirley and I would become glued to the kitchen radio, a Fada multi-band table model. We listened to WHAI in Greenfield and its morning news reporter, Graden Sprague, hoping to hear him announce, "No school in

Ashfield." Later on, Miss Florence Haberle usually would verify this in her 15 minute news of Shelburne Falls and vicinity. We were often devastated to hear that Greenfield, Turners Falls and Shelburne Falls were canceling school, but Ashfield, with its heavier snow but hardier folk, was not!

First Grade (1947 – 1948). Mrs. Ethel Williams, our neighbor up the road in Apple Valley, was the teacher. Russell Williams found it weird at first that it was "Mrs. Williams" at school but still "Aunt Ethel" at home. We had lockers at one side of the cavernous room, where we stored our hats and boots, along with half-eaten sandwiches and other things. We each had a wooden chair and desk, under the top of which we could store books and papers – and those half-eaten sandwiches and other stuff we hadn't yet moved to the lockers.

Mrs. Williams had Janie Field, Betty Mislak and me move our desks to the back of the room. None of us understood why at the time. Janie and I had much in common, though we didn't realize it at the time – her dad, a young farmer like my Dad, had died suddenly, too, not long after she was born. She was indeed smart, smart enough to skip second grade and go right to third.

For recess we went out to play on the big playground behind the school. There was a swing, probably a two or three seat swing set, and a long slide. And there were several acres of playground out back.

Second Grade (1948 – 1949). Our teacher was Mrs. Vivian Fuller, whose career spanned many years at Ashfield Consolidated Schools. We were joined (in the same classroom, that is) with the third grade.

Janie Field, whose whole family was musical, was learning to play the violin, and one day at recess, she played it for us. I was thrilled! It sounded so beautiful!

Mrs. Fuller organized a special Thanksgiving feast for the class. Mothers had to make something for us to bring in and share. Each of us had to dress like someone who would have attended the first Thanksgiving at Plymouth Plantation. I was dressed as a native American.

We second graders carved pumpkins for Halloween that year. While everybody else carved spooky looking goblins and other Halloween faces, I, even then one to suck up, took some of Mother's ever-present cotton batting[17] and made a Santa Claus pumpkin.

Third Grade (1949 – 1950). Mrs. Brooks was our teacher. This was the year I decided to begin the Straight Arrow[18] club. I asked Mrs. Brooks' permission, and announced I was starting it up. To become a member, all my classmates had to do to join was to give me a Shredded Wheat box top and a dime! The club didn't last long; I may have been the only member.

Fourth Grade (1950 – 1951). Fourth grade was generally a bummer. Miss Virginia Rice (no relation, as far as I know, to my grandmother, Ethel (Rice) Bates) was the teacher. She was recently out of college. She was not above a little corporal punishment on occasion, and I remember once she grabbed me by the tip of my chin to bring me face to face with her, and her fingernails raised welts. I wasn't the only one she picked on.

For a while, Miss Rice had us do a "show and tell" early each morning, and Joe Labelle brought in a very small but very live bat. The bat was in a

---

17 Mother had lots of it on hand to cover the Vicks Vaporub or Musterole poultices she attacked us with at the slightest hint of a cold.

18 "Straight Arrow" was a radio program and comic book hero in which rancher Steve Adams, helped by his faithful buddy, Packy, goes to his secret cave and slips into his Comanche persona and rides off on his Palomino, Fury, to right wrongs and bring evil-doers to justice. Straight Arrow was my hero, maybe even more so than the Lone Ranger! The radio program was sponsored by Nabisco Shredded Wheat, and Nabisco's commercials offered all sorts of valuable Straight Arrow treasures which you could get by sending Nabisco a dime and a top from a Shredded Wheat box.

Nabisco went a step further to merchandise its Straight Arrow character. Shredded Wheat came in a cardboard box containing three layers of three "biscuits". Each level was separated by a piece of cardboard. For several years beginning in 1949 the cardboard separators were imprinted with Fred Meagher's cartooned items of Indian lore – presented by my hero, Straight Arrow! Shirley and I collected them, colored them, traded them, and just generally treasured them.

shoebox and when Joe lifted the lid to get the little critter out of the box - you guessed it - the bat flitted away.

Miss Rice started shrieking, and some of the kids did as well. The little bat, with all that noise, kept circling higher and higher around the classroom. It finally lit on the molding at the top of the classroom wall. When Frank Carter, the custodian, got a ladder and climbed up to remove it, the little bugger flitted off to another piece of molding. I never knew how they finally got the bat out of the room, but it was gone the next morning.

What did we do at recess? Most of the time, we boys ran around the very large playground. In spring as the snow melted a bunch of us junior engineers built pretty elaborate mud dams to slow the water as it melted and ran toward Bronson Avenue. My fingers got so cold a couple times that I was unable to grasp a pencil during the next class.

Fifth Grade (1951 – 1952). Our teacher was Miss Dorothy Laughlin. Our class was alone this year, housed in the first floor room at the foot of the stairs near the cafeteria. This was the year in which I was out for much of December and January with Scarlet Fever.

Miss Laughlin loved me. She was a large woman who gave big smothering hugs. If ever there was a teacher's pet, it was me that year. She certainly cut me a lot of slack. One time I hadn't quite finished an art project the class was working on in time for a spelling quiz, so I painted (hand lettered) the spelling answers while I finished the far more interesting art project. She laughed, and I thought I was *so* clever!

Sixth Grade (1952 – 1953). Mr. Robert Denesha was our sixth grade teacher. We were coupled with the fifth graders this year. This was the fall in which Russ Williams contracted polio, a factor that sort of hung over us for at least the first part of the year, as it seemed so unfair that one of *us* should be so afflicted.

This was the first year I remember having gym as a class. Mr. Denesha tried to teach us soccer.

Adolescence began to emerge in earnest, and with it for some of us boys came a kind of bravado, a need to impress the girls. While many of us could contain our behavior, some could not. The Bennett twins, Raymond and Robert, were often the least well-behaved and spent many hours at Principal Armand Guarino's office. Barry Graves, one of the fifth graders, was a cut-up, too. He, too, became a frequent visitor at Mr. Guarino's office.

In June we had a year-end class outing at our farm.

In sixth grade, we had to write a paper about the Constitution or the Bill of Rights. It was a real bear, perhaps the hardest assignment ever in grade school, perhaps because it was so boring to this sixth grader!

Principal Armand Guarino and his family were friendly with Ralph and Martha Townsley. Uncle Ralph was chairman of the School Committee for several years. Mr. Guarino gave a collie named Smoky to Ralph when the dog became too big for his daughters to play with. Smoky was a handsome dog. Ralph had hopes of making a cow dog out of Smoky, but Smoky never figured out what he was supposed to do.

Recess time? The country was immersed in the Korean War at the time, so we boys were soldiers dug in to our foxholes behind the stone wall that ran along one side of the playground. More than once we were a little tardy coming back from lunch.

Fifth and sixth grade outing at Townsley's.
Author's Photo.

Seventh Grade (1953 – 1954). Mr. Joseph Kosiorek was our teacher. He taught seventh and eighth grade, together in the second floor room adjacent to the principal's office. He had a good sense of humor and laughed often, and in general, the year was fun.

In preparation for Memorial Day, we were to learn "It's a Grand Old Flag", the Irving Berlin classic, to sing it at the Memorial Day pageant. Mr. Kosiorek undertook to teach us the song, as best he could remember it, as a surprise for the music teacher. Mrs. Cowell, the music teacher was stunned, especially at a couple of measures in which Mr. Kosiorek's memory had failed him and the tune he conjured up certainly wasn't Berlin's.

This was the last year that I sang soprano. As we practiced "Grand Old Flag" and others during the year, I often was near enough to Janie Field, clearly a soprano, to be able to lean on her for the right notes.

Mr. Kosiorek taught us English grammar. I was amazed to find that the English language actually had a structure, that there were rules and they made sense. This future engineer could confidently parse a sentence! It was so cool!

Mr. Kosiorek once had some sort of beef with the Springfield *Republican* newspaper, the substance of which we never knew. It resulted in a class-wide homework assignment in which each student was to proofread a couple of pages from the paper and highlight all the grammatical and spelling errors. As I remember, we didn't find many.

Gym in seventh grade sometimes consisted of marching out on the playground. With hormones beginning to rage, I came to enjoy marching, especially when lined up behind some of the girls.

At recess that fall the boys played touch football. Mr. Kosiorek quarterbacked one team and Brister Gray led the other. As the nerdy kid on the team nobody expected me to do much, and I didn't disappoint! Sure enough, when Mr. Kosiorek sent me out to catch a pass, I usually fell down before I caught the ball.

Eighth Grade (1954 – 1955). Mr. Donald Perkins was the teacher. It was just us eighth graders in the second floor room facing Bronson Avenue, adjacent to the back stairs. In fact it was then the only classroom facing Bronson Avenue. Construction of an addition to the school began that year, and the noise often interrupted classroom activities.

As I look back, my impression is that Mr. Perkins was not an especially good teacher. Yet as I sit here now, I can't really think of any examples that would substantiate such a condemnation. Curious, too, is the fact that I can think of very few items of interest that took place in eighth grade.

I wrote a play as an eighth grader about the death of Abraham Lincoln. Ray Bennett was Lincoln. Fittingly, like President Lincoln he was too tall for the "death bed" (from the school nurse's office) to which we carried him. Russ Williams was the narrator.

Several of us eighth grade boys were 'recruited' into the high school chorus that year. The school principal, Mr. Joyce, as I remember, barged into our classroom, and said something like, "You, you and you," pointing to a half dozen of us, "come with me!"

He marched us next door into the unfinished cavern of a room then being built, and presented us to Mrs. Cowell with, "Here, these are some Tenors and Basses who just volunteered!"

I attended only a couple of rehearsals, and thoroughly hated every second. I found whatever excuse I could so as not to practice or perform. My voice was doing somersaults that year, and it seldom did what I hoped it might. It was perhaps the only time I ever sang tenor, albeit a weak, adenoidal and nasal tenor, and I before long bottomed out as a lifelong bass.

High School

Sanderson Academy, Ashfield's public four-year high school, had about seventy-five students in all four years. Ashfield Consolidated Schools, grades one through eight, were housed with the high school in one big building on Buckland Road. There was no kindergarten or preschool at the time. On paper we were the Sanderson Rams, though there was no great effort to make us act like male sheep. Our school colors were maroon and white ("wine" and white, actually).

There were ten in my Class of 1959: Bob Bates, Bill Craft, Tom Cranston, Ed Dufresne, Betty Mislak, Dick Pease, Dan Phelps, Nancy Rowe, Joe Valliere and Russ Williams.

Teachers and Staff.

As I compare notes with others, we had some uncommonly good teachers at Sanderson. Without doubt, the best teacher I ever had the pleasure of experiencing, at any level, was Mrs. Louise Sears! She was the high school math teacher during all four years I was at Sanderson, and that meant she taught everything from four-function arithmetic to nearly college-level trigonometry. Mrs. Sears was patient, firm, fair, and taught with an appropriate level of seriousness and humor. Later when I became a teacher, it was Mrs. Sears whom I tried to emulate.

Frank Carter was the only custodian during the dozen years I was at Sanderson. He lived in the space beneath the gymnasium, or so it seemed. He had to have had the patience of a saint to have suffered us little terrors – and to keep coming back for more every year.

Freshman Year (1955 – 1956).

Mrs. Connie Rice was our Biology teacher. We got to look at all sorts of weird stuff under microscopes and try to draw what we observed. Some of us had better luck with it than others.

I took French 1 this year. Our teacher was Mr. Bascetta. I don't ever remember hearing anyone mention his first name, although he once told us he was a Sicilian Italian – and his accent certainly wasn't a New Englander's. Much later a friend commented, "Bob, you're the first New Englander I ever heard who spoke French with a Sicilian accent!"

In Phys Ed coach Bunting found some boxing gloves. He matched me with Barry Graves as he and I were about the same size. I never got a punch off while Barry pummeled me! Mr. Bunting stopped the bout after about the longest thirty seconds I ever knew.

Sophomore Year (1956 – 1957).

The Sanderson Yearbook this year provided us with a little laughter. In a section highlighting "Best…" and "Most…," Cynthia Field and I are pictured poring over a stack of books under the caption "Best Dancers." I can't speak for Janie, but that was about the furthest from the truth for me. On closer look, "Best Dancers" were supposed to be Nelson "Pete" Howes and Fay Cranson.

Our parents insisted we take dancing lessons. Izzy Hand, who lived in town, assisted occasionally by her husband, Skip, led the class. Among her students were Bill and Sue Craft, Marianne Roberts, Shirley and me. Classes were held in the basement of Hand's new home in town.

It was here I learned that dancing with Sue or Marianne was very different from dancing with Shirley: dancing with your sister may be fun, but there's no future to it. There wasn't much future in dancing with Marianne or Sue either, as it turned out.

Later in the year the Parent Teachers Association, of which my mom was Chairman, organized a Baby Sitters School. Bill and I, along with a dozen or more others, sat in on the class. It ran for several late afternoons. The thing that made it memorable for me was that one afternoon we got to change the diapers of a live squirming baby! Marion Gray brought her infant son for one of the classes so that we could get some experience with a real live infant.

Junior Year (1957 – 1958).

Our English teacher this year, Miss Helen Barber, was an interesting young woman. She appeared to know her subject pretty well and she loved English Literature. Miss Barber was something of an eccentric. For one, she wore a uniform – a medium gray suit (skirt and jacket), a light gray high necked blouse, wrinkly cotton hose (not nylons) and "sensible" shoes. She never smiled, either, except maybe just the hint of a smile when she rhapsodized over Shakespeare, Keats and Shelley. As students, we focused on Miss Barber's eccentricities instead of the subject matter, and that undermined whatever good she was trying to accomplish. As a result, she was near tears on several occasions at our acting up, and all in all, was not an effective teacher.

Yet it was around this time that I began to write creatively. In a sense, this book may have sprung from at least a few seeds sown in Miss Barber's classroom that year.

The social highlight was the Junior Prom. We classmates worked for weeks designing and making the decorations for the high school gymnasium. For this timid youngster, working up nerve enough to ask a girl to the dance was a feat. I was horribly shy and nervous. I screwed up my courage and invited Nancy Rowe to the Junior Prom, and amazingly, she accepted! Nancy was pretty and petite with a killer figure. I couldn't figure why she went with me, but I never had enough confidence to consider she actually might have even *liked* me.

The prom meant renting a tux in Greenfield and getting a corsage from Shaw Florist in Shelburne Falls. Transportation was a problem - I didn't yet have my license to drive, so Mother had to drive us - I was mortified! I was scared, too: here I was, nerdy little Bobbie Bates, who through some weird quirk of fate was out on a date with the nicest girl in the whole school! I was terrified! I don't remember a whole lot about the evening, except that we sat a lot and we didn't talk much. I never saw Nancy after high school.

Senior Year (1958 – 1959).

Russ Williams, Bill Craft and I were Mrs. Sears' Trigonometry Class this year. We were so puzzled at the homework that we decided to get together on the telephone to do our homework. I'd call Russ (he and I were on the same party line) and ask him to pick up the phone in a minute or so. Then I'd call Bill in Ashfield, Russ would join in, and we'd be done pretty quickly. It didn't take Mrs. Sears long to catch on - we'd all made the same mistakes! But though she frowned on it, we weren't forbidden to do it.

On our senior class trip to Washington, DC, in 1959 (we joined up with the seniors from Worthington), some of the girls came over to our boys' hotel room for an evening of kissing and heavy petting. Some of us were not involved - and were a little nervous about the whole deal! Mrs. Sears, our chaperone, found us out and was livid. When we got back to Sanderson the whole senior class was given a suspended suspension.

For graduation there was a Baccalaureate Service at the Congregational Church, and the graduation exercises were held at the Town Hall. Mother had a broken leg at the time, but she clumped up the many stairs at Town Hall so she wouldn't miss my graduation exercises.

Extracurricular Activities.

Sanderson Academy was small enough that we had only four sports, baseball, softball, boys' basketball and girls' basketball. For the time that I attended we never had even close to a championship team in any sport. One baseball game at arch rival Williamsburg was typical: we lost 20 – 0. But another time, at Hardwick, pitcher Bill Thayer tossed a dandy game, and though I don't remember if we won, we were close.

Sanderson had cheerleaders for boys' basketball. Betty Mislak and Nancy Rowe, the two girls from my class, were among them. Betty remembers, "We wore satin long full-sleeved and snug cuffed blouses with a maroon corduroy mid thigh full skirt, white socks and white sneakers."

Much as I loved the game (and still do), I was not a good baseball player, so I sat on the bench and kept the scorebook. I was even worse at basketball, so I kept the scorebook there, too. Both functions required me to phone the results to the Greenfield Recorder-Gazette, which made me feel important.

There were several dances besides the Prom at the high school gymnasium each year. Typically of the time, the boys sat and goofed off along one wall and the girls sat and giggled along the opposite wall. In desperation, some of the girls danced together, and the boys stared at them fondly.

There had been very popular square dances at the Ashfield Town Hall for many years. People came from all around. I was astounded years later as an acquaintance in Nashua remarked, "You're from Ashfield?! I used to go square dancing there every weekend! Do they still have them?" Sadly, by the time I was of going-to-dances age the regular square dances had been discontinued.

With as small a school as Sanderson, the annual senior class play sometimes had to use a few Juniors. In "Hot Ice" in my junior year I played "Sharp", a private detective. In my senior year we put on "Let's Be Congenial," a comedy in three acts by Paul Pray, as the 1959 senior class play. Thanks, English teacher Margaret (Peg) Lavallee for the reminder of the play name. All I can remember about the play was that in one scene I got to kiss Lorna Wilde, a Junior, one of the foxiest girls in the school.

Though certainly not a school activity, some of us played poker regularly. Beginning in my Senior year and for many years afterwards a bunch of us played almost every Friday. The games were held at various homes. Russ Williams was a regular, Joe LaBelle was usually there, as were Carl and Wendell Greenman. Bill Thayer and Bill Craft sat in sometimes. It was really high stakes: penny ante mostly, and none of us except Russell ever came out very far ahead.

Chapter 10
Hunting and Fishing

Having a couple brooks nearby made growing up on the farm a lot of fun. As a toddler you could see the big splashes when you threw rocks, as a ten-year-old you could find strange bugs and worms and the dreaded huge brown spiders that lurked beside the brook. Later it was a place to launch your navy, and build a dam, and still later, find an island in the pasture to claim as your own.

We fished the brook fairly often until we were old enough to go hunting. I still remember catching my first trout. It was down at Gramp Nelson's, in a little hole in the edge of the brook right near the end of his garden. I was 7 or 8. Gramp may have been feeding it for a while, because it was the easiest catch I ever had. He had me drop a line with an earthworm on the hook into the hole and, as I recall, almost in the same motion, I pulled out the trout.

The trout we caught were 10" or less, most in the 6" to 8" range. Landing a foot-long trout could make you legendary, and it was rumored that Charlie Groff had gotten one once. He loomed large in my list of fishing heroes.

Another hero who loomed large was Jordan Monohon. Jordan, then living at Scott's up the road, was a frequent visitor to the Townsley farm in the early 1950s. He took me aside and showed me that you need to sneak up on trout. Trout are wary and cautious, and when you boldly walk up to the edge of the brook and toss your line in, chances are any worthwhile trout has darted into hiding. And what do you know, he was right! It was another life lesson: you get/find/learn a lot more if you're patient and careful in your approach.

Steve Greenman, Russ Williams and I drove up the Brown Road one evening in my Volkswagen to where the beavers had rebuilt the dam we blew out a year or so earlier. Steve was still a teenager. In the meantime, the Valiton brothers had stocked the pond with bullheads ("catfish" to some folks), and the fishing could be good if things went right.

There was still enough dusk left to see our way down to the pond. We left Russ at the shore and Steve and I clambered through some heavy brush around to the beaver dam. After a while the mosquitoes began to attack us.

We weren't having much luck fishing, so Steve and I gave up and began our trek back to the car. It was dark, real murky, with no moon. Under the trees it would have been extra dark anyway.

We trudged through the brush, stumbling over the rocks and tripping into trees, until after a while Steve spoke up, "Hey, Batesy, isn't that the dam?" pointing not too far from where we were. Smart-assed kid! I didn't want to admit it, but he was right, we'd come about full circle back to where we started a half hour earlier. We hollered for Russ to see if he had started back to the car. And when he didn't answer, I began to get a little concerned!

But during the silence while listening for his answer, we could hear, very faintly, the sound of music. It didn't sound like anything heavenly, so it must be my car radio. With that now as a homing beacon, we got back to the car in short order. Russ had heard us getting ready to head up from the dam, and he got back up the hill to the car quickly. When we didn't show up for a while, he opened the sunroof and turned on the radio. I didn't admit to Steve for years that I had been lost, but he knew right away! Boy, was I thankful to hear that radio! Thanks again, Russ!

I had two .22 caliber rifles as a youngster. My first .22, a single shot Stevens, was given to me by Gramp Nelson. He had once shot a fox with it from an upstairs window in his old applehouse, where Steve and Diane Greenman's house is now. The fox had been marauding the range toward Townsley's where Gramp had his spring pullets, and Gramp shot it right in its eye. We marveled at that, and Nannie and my mom kidded him about his prowess.

I bagged my first woodchuck in the orchard just below the trefoil piece with Gramp's old Stevens. I was so excited that I carted that little woodchuck carcass down to Gramp's to show it off. Gramp showed me how to skin and gut it, and Mother cooked it. There isn't much left to a woodchuck after you cook it. It tastes like squirrel, raccoon and other small game, and has lots of tiny bones but not much meat.

My second .22 was a tube fed, bolt action JC Higgins (Sears, Roebuck) I bought from Russ Williams. Russ bought the rifle new from Sears. It had a telescopic sight and a leather sling, but proved to be too cumbersome to carry with his crutches. Russ and I test-fired the rifle, using rests and supports, at a nutmeg tin target set out about 50 yards. When we put three shots into that tin - you could literally cover the three bullet holes with a dime - I knew I had to have that rifle.

Another rifle I used from time to time was Ralph's .22 caliber lever-action Marlin. Its action was smooth, as opposed to the jerky action of a bolt action,

A successful hunt! Left to right: Malcolm Clark, Ralph Townsley, Doc Streeter.
Unknown photographer, Martha D. Townsley Collection.

and it had a peep sight. At the time I thought the best idea was to be able to get off lots of shots, quickly, to bag your game. Later I learned what would be a great life lesson: make your first shot your best; not much game is brought down with second or third shots - unless you have a shotgun.

My only shotgun was a break action single-barrel 12 gauge piece whose forearm was only loosely snapped to the barrel, so that often the forearm would come off the gun altogether as you fired it. It was an old piece, and Uncle Ralph, who claimed to have shot his first squirrel with it, had wrapped electrical tape around where the wooden stock joined the metal parts of the shotgun.

Mother and Pres forbade me to go deer hunting, something that in Massachusetts in 1957 meant using a shotgun, until I had actually shot a shotgun once. It was hard to challenge the logic of that requirement, so one October afternoon I set out into the field below Roundtop with the gun, a half-dozen birdshot shells and a soup tin.

I'd heard that a lightweight shotgun had a pretty honest kick, so I bought a special stiff rubber cushion for the butt of the stock. Still nervous about the kick, I decided (and to this day I have no idea what I was thinking) that the kick might not be as bad if I shot from a prone, laying-down position! Still I was worried, so I set the shotgun up on my shoulder, bazooka-style. I cocked the hammer, sighted as best I could down the barrel at the soup tin, pulled the trigger, and Uncle Ralph's old squirrel gun roared!

My first thought was, "Rats! Missed the soup tin!" My second thought was that I had only the gun's forearm in my left hand. Then it dawned on me that the rest of the shotgun was gone! I glanced behind me, and there, tumbling end-over-end toward the applehouse, was that dreaded shotgun!

Deerslayers – but no deer, 1930s. Left to right: Lewis Bates, Glendon Crafts, Wally Doneilo, Mike Warger, A. Doneilo, Frank Eldridge, Willis Thayer and John Krasnoselski.
Unknown photographer, Author's Collection.

After reassembling the forearm to the barrel and, in the privacy of the applehouse, carefully cleaning the mud and grass out of the barrel and out of the hammer mechanism, I concluded there was no other way than to stand up, shoulder that blunderbuss, and let her rip. And when I did, my first thought was, "Yes, YES, I hit the soup tin!!" The forearm had come loose from the barrel again (I electrical-taped it in place later), but I still held the rest of the gun. Not only that, but my shoulder was still intact!

In looking back, I realize God does indeed look after damn fools and neophyte hunters, and that day I surely was both! I *could* have caught my index finger in the trigger guard and dislocated it or torn it off completely! I *could* have severely damaged my right eye when the hammer chamber flew past my head! But I didn't. Thank you again, God!!

By the way, it didn't kick nearly as badly as everybody said it would.

Soon after getting my first hunting license, I went hunting for rabbits or partridges up near "Gramp's" orchard soon after a snowstorm. It was about 15 degrees, sunny and absolutely still. The snow squeaked with each step. Everything all around glistened and sparkled and smelled so clean. All you could hear was the twittering of chickadees and the occasional call of a blue jay. Funny – from my vantage point now more than fifty years later, I can't tell you if I got any game that morning, but the memory of the day is crystal clear!

One December late afternoon, I was deer hunting after school up in the sugar orchard, back when the side hill was open pasture. It was cold and still, and it was late in the afternoon, well on its way to dark. Below me was the farm. The lights were on in the barn. Ralph and Pres were getting ready for milking: one of them was tapping the cover off a forty quart milk can, and it was like a bell. I shivered a bit, and my breath hung in the air before me, but I knew that soon I, too, would be in that barn, and it would be warm and pungent and *home*.

I got lost only once in my life. It was while deer hunting with Malcolm Clark and Wayne Jones in Baptist Corner. It was a foggy day, and the three of us started walking along a ridge, me in the middle and Malcolm and Wayne on either side. After an hour or so I lost sight of both of them, and in the fog, hadn't a clue where I was. Before long I came across Willy Gray; we exchanged greetings, but I didn't let on I was lost. A bit later, I came across Malcolm's pickup and waited there a short time before Malcolm and Wayne returned. Nothing was said about my disappearance, and I certainly didn't volunteer that I'd been lost!

Crows had a reputation of stealing newly planted corn seeds and the like, and so are considered by most farmers to be vermin which should be exterminated as quickly as possible. Whether or not this reputation is deserved is questioned today, as some studies indicate that crows consume way more bugs than seeds. Nonetheless, in the 1950s, crows were fair targets.

Crows are a wily lot. Hunting them can be a challenge, as the crows learn quickly and will be very wary of unusual sounds and sights. A favorite trick, to be used from late June through early August (when fledgling crows leave the nest), takes advantage of crow's instinct to protect their young. The "trick" is a crow call, a small wooden whistle-shaped thing that when you blew it just right you could make it sound just like a young crow in distress. You can use it in a given area only once a season because all the area crows quickly learned that answering the distress call resulted in a shotgun barrage.

One summer afternoon Malcolm Clark, Wayne Jones and I went crow hunting. I was the new kid, never having hunted crows before. I had just bought a new crow call and was anxious to try it out, and off we went, me with Ralph's old 12 gauge shotgun, to a meadow in Plainfield. The three of us backed into a scrub pine well out of sight, and I offered the call to Malcolm so he could show me how to use it.

Well, what a cacophony Malcolm coaxed out of that wooden call! He made the call shriek and squawk, and it sounded for all the world like something or somebody was strangling some poor defenseless baby crow. Before long, way off in the distance, crows began calling one another, and soon, on the horizon you could begin to see many crows warily flying in our direction.

I spotted a single crow, perhaps 300 yards out, flying in my direction. Without any warning to Malcolm or Wayne, I let loose a blast from the 12 gauge. I about startled the crap out of them. The crow did a sudden change of direction and joined the rest of the now sizeable flock fleeing the neighborhood. Malcolm and Wayne didn't say much – they didn't have to. I learned that patience is a virtue, especially while hunting.

Later I put that lesson to use. Hunting alone this time, I called and squawked, just like Malcolm had done, and soon had several trees full of curious and fretful crows. I burst out of the underbrush where I was hiding, and blasted the one shot from that single barrel shotgun. By the time I could reload, perhaps three seconds, the sky was empty and all one could hear was the wind whistling through the pines and the crows calling one another – way off in the distance. But I had managed to slay one of the dreaded flock.

There were no bears in Ashfield in the 1950s. Occasionally you might hear a rumor of one in a neighboring town, but most often it turned out to be somebody's big black dog or just plain fiction. Coyotes were unheard of as well. Wild turkeys had been long gone from the scene by the late 1950s, though they would be successfully re-introduced within a decade. Once in a while there were pheasants which had been stocked by the Rod and Gun Club. Fred Scott tells a funny pheasant-hunting story in his book about how he and his dad were tricked by Ralph Townsley one fall with an old stuffed pheasant.

Woodchucks were considered vermin on the farm, mostly because of their habit of digging burrows, often in the middle of prime hayfields. This raised problems when haying, more so in the old days when a woodchuck hole hidden in the grass could dislocate or break horses' or cows' legs. "Woodchucking" was great training for a fledgling hunter, and the firearm of choice was a .22 caliber rifle, though I sometimes used a 12 gauge shotgun. A favorite place to hunt woodchucks was "the trefoil piece," a field above the blueberry patch where we once had planted a state-of-the-art grass called trefoil.

During the summers as a teen, I'd head off with my .22 soon after supper, hunting for woodchucks. Often I'd head out the lane from the barn, then up the brook next to the orchard, checking out a couple of rock piles and fields along the way. Then I'd walk toward the blueberry patch and the trefoil piece, where there often was a woodchuck along the fence between the orchard and the trefoil piece. Sometimes I'd continue on to Roundtop where there frequently was a woodchuck in the rock piles or the fence between our orchard and Scott's.

Wayne Jones, who summered at Clark's on the opposite side of Apple Valley, came flying into our yard one late afternoon, shouting, "Bob, come on! There's a woodchuck up in the middle of your trefoil piece!"

He saw it clearly from Malcolm and Pauline's, grabbed Richard's old truck and raced down to our farm to alert me. We stealthily walked up through the orchard over the upper stone bridge, then sneaked along under the grown-over fence between the trefoil piece and the orchard. We carefully poked our heads over the fence for a look, and sure enough, that silly woodchuck was still there, about 30 yards away in the middle of the field, munching contentedly on clover and trefoil. Wayne and I each took a shot. When we did, the woodchuck sat up to see what the noise was all about. We each squeezed off another shot, and the woodchuck began to run off toward the edge of the field. We continued to blaze away, and that stupid woodchuck actually had the gall to stop running after a minute and sit up to see if it was safe yet.

The rest of that story? The woodchuck got away, and Ralph, Malcolm and Richard laughed about it for days.

Russell Townsley with a very respectable 9 inch trout!
Martha D. Townsley Photograph

I often walked the route that Wayne and I followed, past the apple house, through the orchard, across the upper stone bridge and to the fence just below the north end of the trefoil piece. Until this point I usually strode along, as there weren't apt to be many woodchucks. But as I reached the trefoil piece my pace slowed as I started looking and listening in earnest. One evening as I crept across the trefoil piece toward the blueberry patch, I heard a woodchuck "whistling" in the near distance.

The only sound I've heard a woodchuck make is a high-pitched whistle-like series of chirps, not unlike the sound a squirrel makes when it's startled. Intended as an alarm to other woodchucks, it's something like, "WHEAP wheap wheapwheapwheap," starting very loud then diminishing in volume to a whisper. A chuck will sit there, on the pile of rocks under the brush in this case, repeating this warning every few seconds until he sees something to send him scurrying into his hole – or until he gets bored.

My attention became focused on a brush-covered rock pile. Somewhere under the brush, the chuck continued his concert. I crept closer, step by careful step, peering into the underbrush, trying to push the leaves aside with my eyes. Soon I was at the very edge of the rocks and brush, and still I couldn't find the woodchuck, nor apparently had he seen me, because the whistling continued. I started to circle the pile, hoping still to see the varmint.

Suddenly, out of the corner of my eye, I caught a movement. Glancing around, there was a fox, hunting for that same woodchuck just as intently as I was, and she, too, was circling the brush pile and creeping right toward me. We saw one another about the same time, and for the briefest moment we stared at one another in surprise. Off she bounded, racing along the edge of the trefoil piece toward the heavier cover as I shouldered my .22, but she was gone before I could squeeze off a shot.

Needless to say, with all the commotion, the woodchuck had scuttled back to its burrow, and neither that red fox nor I were successful that evening.

The sun by now had long since dropped over the saddle between Pumpkin Hill and the sugar orchard. I swept one more gaze across the valley from Scotts to the left, then to the right toward Clark's new east orchard and beyond. The last rays of sun painted the top of bald Putt's Hill in Buckland, and the evening birds and insects began their symphony. It was time to go home.

Epilogue
What Is It About Ashfield?

Why are we drawn to the Ashfields of the world? What is the attraction not only with the real and tangible Ashfields of not so long ago, but the Ashfields each of us see so vividly in our imagination? There is a lure, a fascination with "coming home" to sights, sounds and smells which are familiar, of reaching back to a life that was simpler - to *Ashfield*.

Current Ashfield residents cast an amused raised eyebrow at us starry-eyed tourists. They say we remember only the good parts. They say we forgot the reality of frigid winters and frozen water pipes, of stifling summers and parched gardens, of late frosts or hail that killed the apple crop, of brucellosis that felled the prize cow in the meager herd. And they may be right.

It's hard to define what pulls us, because there's no one thing, but lots of little things. For me, the answer is easy - my son and his family live here. But that's only part of it.

What brings us back? What's the attraction? For one thing, it's the town, a post-card picture nestled in the heart of the Berkshires. It's the town hall with its Wrenn-inspired steeple. It's the two churches, still pristine and white, still vibrant and active. It's the hills and valleys, and Ashfield Lake, where we learned to swim.

For another thing, it's the people. People share a genuine concern for one another. They're people who really care and who are unafraid to reach out and help one another. It's old folks sharing values and relevant history. It's Moms and Dads struggling to balance earning a living with caring for youngsters. It's bright-eyed children, full of promise, each one an affirmation of God's hope for you and me.

Bill Craft touched on it when he observed, "I think, as we get older, we begin to feel a need to connect." He's right. There's a need to find our place in life's continuum. There's a need to be part of something that's right and important. And there was and still is a lot that's right in all our Ashfields.

Bob Bates
Nashua, New Hampshire
May 2009

Index